THE LIFE AND TIMES OF
LEPKE BUCHALTER

THE LIFE AND TIMES OF
LEPKE BUCHALTER

America's Most Ruthless
Labor Racketeer

Paul R. Kavieff

BARRICADE BOOKS

Fort Lee, New Jersey

Published by Barricade Books Inc.
185 Bridge Plaza North
Suite 308-A
Fort Lee, NJ 07024

www.barricadebooks.com

A copy of the Library of Congress Cataloging-in-Publication Data is
available upon request from the Library of Congress.

ISBN 1-56980-291-2

First Printing
Manufactured in the United States of America

I would like to dedicate this book with love to my soul mate,
Rita Davis Kramer.

Contents

Acknowledgments

I would like to thank the many people who both helped and encouraged me to write this book. I would like to thank, as always, Penelope Morris, owner of the P. A. Morris Co., for her help in editing and creating a hard copy of this work; my friends and colleagues at Wayne State University Engineering Unit; Dr. Kenneth Cobb, director of the Municipal Archives of the City of New York; H. G. Manos; the personnel of the photographic division at the U.S. Library of Congress; Allan May; Georgia E. Wilder; a special thanks to Jeff Nordstedt, vice president of Barricade Books; Barbara and Jeffrey Rice; Patterson Smith; Allan Wilson, senior editor at Barricade Books; the F.B.I. Freedom of Information Section; the Burton Collection and General Information Section of the Detroit Public Library; and Carole and Lyle Stuart, publishers and owners of Barricade Books.

Introduction

It was always the eyes. Those wide, soft doelike eyes that hid the piracy and the murder that lurked behind them. This physical feature was the only thing about Louis "Lepke" Buchalter that distinguished him from any other legitimate businessman. At five feet, seven inches tall, he was not an imposing figure, and yet at the height of his power during the first half of the twentieth century, he ruled over a mob of almost three hundred men, all hardened criminals. These gangsters were specialists in union manipulation, extortion, labor racketeering, industrial sabotage, and murder.

Evaluated in his childhood as an average student and with only an elementary-school education, Buchalter in his prime manipulated some 250 criminal ventures, kept his eye on at least 200 straw bosses, a corps of accountants and bookkeepers, and a staff of irresponsible triggermen, strong arms, and industrial saboteurs. Lepke's personal staff was comprised of some of the most brutal professional assassins in the history of the New York underworld. These thugs included men such as Emanuel "Mendy" Weiss, Charles "the Bug" Workman, and Allie "Tick Tock" Tannenbaum. Legend has it that Tannenbaum was called "Tick Tock" because he dispatched his victims with the casual regularity of a wall clock's beat.

Lepke's name was hardly known to the public in 1935 when he and his partner, Jacob "Gurrah" Shapiro, ruled over the New York garment industry as absolutely as Russian czars. This was an industry that at the time manufactured 75 percent of the clothing worn by Americans. In the underworld, it was a different story. "Lepke," as Buchalter liked his friends to call him, was recognized by his fellow mob bosses as one of the most-powerful underworld leaders in the country. His advice was often sought by other gangsters on the make, and his decisions in intermob disputes were considered final. "I don't ask questions," said one Lepke associate. "I just obey. It would be more healthier." He was sometimes referred to as Judge Louis by his underworld colleagues, who respected his advice and counsel.

To his wife, Betty, and his stepson, Harold, he was a loving husband and a doting father. He seldom raised his voice or swore. He spent most nights at home with his family in their Central Park West apartment. He was the complete antithesis of the powerful mob boss. With an almost apologetic manner, Lepke ordered the murders of recalcitrant union officials or potential witnesses. This was some sixty to one hundred murders by the end of his career. "No witnesses, no indictments" was one of Buchalter's favorite expressions.

By the early 1930s, Buchalter had established a working arrangement with the Brooklyn underworld combination, later dubbed Murder Inc. This enforcement arm of the New York mob worked under the protection of the Mangano crime family in Brooklyn. Murder Inc. killers were put on a yearly retainer by Lepke to do some of the dirty work that he did not want his personal staff involved in.

Labor racketeering in the New York garment industry evolved from a sideline business for Lower East Side gangs to a major underworld enterprise between 1900 and 1930. The man chiefly responsible for organized crime's shift from labor slugging to the sophisticated control of key needle-trade unions in the New York garment industry was Louis "Lepke" Buchalter. The evolution of labor racketeering in the New York needle trades is essentially the story of the rise and fall of Lepke Buchalter.

The whole arrangement seemed foolproof until Special Prosecutor Thomas E. Dewey set his sights on Lepke and Gurrah's garment-center empire in 1936. By the late thirties, both men had become fugitives to avoid pending state and federal indictments. While on the lam, Lepke directed a reign of terror against potential Dewey witnesses. Federal law-enforcement pressure finally caused underworld leaders to force Buchalter to surrender to the feds on a prearranged deal that in reality was never made. Sentenced to fourteen years in prison on a federal drug-trafficking conviction in 1939, Lepke believed he would not be turned over to the state of New York to be tried on pending indictments. All of that changed in the spring of 1940 when Abe "Kid Twist" Reles became a state witness in the prosecution of Murder Inc. cases.

From a humble childhood on Manhattan's Lower East

Side, Lepke would rise from being a package thief and pushcart terrorist to one of the most-powerful gang lords in U.S. history. His unraveling was due more to his own paranoia than to mistakes he made in ruling his racket empire.

—Paul R. Kavieff
Royal Oak, Michigan

1 The Early Years

"Going back to the very beginning you wonder how Louis Buchalter ever wound up that way." [1]

—Burton Turkus
Murder Inc. prosecutor

L ouis Buchalter was born into a world on the brink of the modern age. He was born in a dark and over-crowded tenement flat on Manhattan's Lower East Side on February 6, 1897. The youngest of seven children (some accounts say eleven) and small in stature, as a child his mother lovingly called him "Lepkeleh," a Yiddish diminutive meaning "Little Louis." [2] The Buchalters were typical of the penniless Russian Jewish immigrant families who settled on the Lower East Side in the 1890s. [3] Buchalter's father, Barnett, operated a small retail hard-ware store on Essex Street not far from the family's tene-ment home at 217 Henry. [4] Both parents had been wid-owed at an early age. Rose Buchalter arrived in New York with her first husband, Solomon Kauver, and four chil-dren in 1892. As a result, Louis had two half-brothers and two half-sisters. Three more children were born out of the union of Rose and Barnett Buchalter: Emmanual Buchalter, Isadore Buchalter, and Louis. [5]

Louis was reared in a good home by poor, but respectable parents who struggled to provide their children with the necessities of life. Lepke grew up on his own. His parents were too preoccupied with their economic problems to give their children any individual attention or constructive supervision. Yet out of all the chaos of their childhood, only Lepke turned to a life of crime.[6]

Nothing in Lepke's childhood indicated his criminal capacity. People who knew Louis Buchalter as a child described him as soft voiced, soft eyed, and shy—a rather ordinary child who, according to one contemporary who knew him well, "should have turned out better."[7]

Lepke entered Public School No. 75 on the Lower East Side when he was six years old. He transferred to Public School No. 62 in the sixth grade. In 1910 when Lepke was thirteen, his father died, and the family home on Henry Street was broken up. Two married half-sisters and an older half-brother moved to Denver, Colorado, where Lepke's half-brother became a rabbi and a university professor. For a short time, in a desperate attempt to make ends meet, Rose Buchalter peddled herring from door to door on Henry Street.[8]

Lepke, his mother, and two brothers moved to the Williamsburg section of Brooklyn. During the ensuing two years, Buchalter attended Public School No. 94 where, as in the schools he had previously attended, he attained good marks for conduct, studies, and attendance. He was fifteen years old when he graduated from Public School No. 94 on June 28, 1912. During this time, there was nothing to indicate that Lepke was a behavior problem. He was considered a quiet, well-behaved youth of average intelligence. Soon after graduating from elementary school, Lepke's personality showed signs of change. In 1912, he was arrested for participating in a gang fight in lower Manhattan. He was arraigned in Children's Court and later discharged.[9]

Rose Buchalter may or may not have known that by the time Lepke was fifteen, he was a very tough kid who spent most of his time across the river on the Lower East Side where he committed petty thefts, extortions, and other random acts of violence. His mother still may not have given up on Louis. What we would regard today as delinquent behavior was considered conventional in Lower East Side life then.[10]

Sensing trouble, Lepke's older half-brother in Denver offered to send funds for his continued education, but Louis did not return to school in the fall of 1912. Instead, he found a job as a delivery boy making $3 a week. He turned over a major portion of his wages to his mother, who earned a meager income serving kosher food in her small Brooklyn apartment to elderly widows sent to her by a local rabbi.[11]

Lepke showed a marked personality change at this time. When he lost his job as a delivery boy, he chose to remain unemployed. He became more independent and spent his leisure time in the Lower East Side neighborhood where the Buchalter family had previously lived. There he loitered on street corners and frequented poolrooms where he came into contact with underworld characters who began to influence him. Emulating the conduct of his ill-chosen associates, Buchalter made no intensive effort to find employment, preferring instead to secure his money by joining his companions in their exploits as purse snatchers and package thieves.

It was during this time that Lepke's life choices changed. He began to see the world through the gangster's eye. By this value system, mankind fits into distinct categories: wolves and lambs, predators and victims, winners and losers, deceivers and deceived, the elite and the rabble. It is the elite few who grasp this truth and possess the courage and energy to act upon it. What distinguishes gangsters from the rest of the elite-capitalists, politicians, law enforcers, and all the others who are successful in their legitimate vocations is that gangsters are aboveboard, transparently honest with themselves.[12]

In late 1912, Rose Buchalter left Brooklyn to live with Lepke's half-brother in Denver. Lepke was directed to live with a relative in Brooklyn, but after his mother moved west, he lived in furnished rooms on the Lower East Side. It was during this period that Lepke met and became fast friends with another delinquent two years his senior. Jacob Shapiro, better known in the underworld as "Gurrah Jake," was born in Minsk, Russia, in 1895 and was brought to the Lower East Side by his parents in 1907.[13] The hulking, slow-witted Shapiro earned his underworld nickname of "Gurrah" because that was the way the words came out when he muttered his favorite expression, "Gurrah da here." Translated this meant "get out of here," which was usually accompanied by a blow or a kick.[14] Another account claimed that Gurrah was the contraction of the cry sent up by harassed pushcart peddlers when Shapiro came to raid their stock or cash. They would let loose with an anguished "Gurrah here, Jake," the nearest they could come to "get out of here, Jake."[15]

While demoralizing neighborhood influences were without question contributing factors in Lepke's evolving conduct and later criminal career, it is significant that none of the other Buchalter children reared in the same environment came into conflict with the law. Lepke's brother, Emmanual, became a dentist, Isadore Buchalter a pharmacist, his half-brother in Denver a rabbi and university professor, and an older half-sister a schoolteacher. What did Lepke become? "The most dangerous criminal in the U.S.," said F.B.I. Director J. Edgar Hoover. "The worst industrial racketeer in America," declared District Attorney Thomas E. Dewey in 1937.[16]

Working in partnership with Shapiro, Lepke became a package thief and a pushcart terrorist on the Lower East Side. The teenagers extorted small amounts of money from pushcart peddlers for protection against merchandise damage.[17] Lepke also ran errands and did favors for older, established underworld figures.

When Lepke dipped his toes into crime, the area was lively, with almost nightly gunplay. There were many big shots for whom an ambitious kid could do favors and odd jobs. Lepke lived on the fringes of big-time crime and cautiously began to feel his way.[18] He graduated from pushcart terrorist into loft burglar in 1915. His first arrest as an adult came on September 2, 1915, when he was arrested in Manhattan and charged with burglary and felonious assault. The case was discharged by a grand jury on September 29, 1915. Buchalter was arrested for the second time on January 12, 1916, again charged with burglary and again discharged.

On February 29, 1916, Lepke and an accomplice were arrested in Bridgeport, Connecticut, and charged with theft. According to a later report by State Attorney General Galen A. Carter dated May 17, 1917, Louis Buchalter was charged with the theft of property valued at $500. He reportedly came to Bridgeport with an accomplice for the purpose of stealing. Buchalter and his companion stole two suitcases containing jewelry samples that were left by a salesman outside the door of a Bridgeport store.

Convicted of theft in Bridgeport, Lepke received an indeterminate sentence at the Connecticut State Reformatory at Cheshire on May 16, 1916. He was admitted May 18, 1916, as number 517 and released on parole July 12, 1917. On July 23, 1917, he left the area and returned to New York City. A warrant was issued for violation of parole, but never executed. The following data was entered on Buchalter's fingerprint card for the State Reformatory at Cheshire, Connecticut, on August 18, 1916. For Louis Buchalter:

Height: 5'6?"

Weight: 152? lbs.

Beard: dark

Residence: 33 Hillhouse Ave., Bridgeport, CT

Sister: Mrs. Bilthick, 355 E. 141st Street, New York, N.Y. (no further information regarding this alleged sister is available at this time)

Heredity: Excellent father and mother. Father died in 1910, mother is refined and well educated; 1-sister is a schoolteacher; 1-brother a rabbi with a Ph.D. degree; 1-stepbrother a dentist; 2-uncles dentists; 1-uncle a druggist; a cousin specializing in Psychology at Columbia at present.

Home: Lived with mother after father's death. Mother went to live in Colorado and inmate went to live with sister. Home conditions the best.

Physical: normal

Dental: normal

School: 5 grades in 10 years

Vocational: steady work as a stock clerk in clothing store owned by family

Habits: good

Delinquency: Two previous arrests for burglary discharged. Present arrest, steals valise in Bridgeport because he was out of funds. Inmate is a clean cut intelligent Hebrew, who led a normal life in spite of little supervision until August 1916. Then worked for an uncle who owned the Orpheum at Savin Rock, who reduced his wages to 8 dollars a week. This he did not like and went back to New York and got in with a bad crowd doing petty jobs. His delinquency is probably the result of mental conflict coupled with companions. Outlook is excellent.

Ability: Good

While at this institution subject Buchalter's only correspondence was recorded as Phillip Kauver, Atlantic Hotel, Bridgeport, Connecticut. Kauver is a brother.[19]

Soon after Lepke returned to New York in July 1917, he was arrested again. On September 28, 1917, he was arrested and charged with grand larceny second degree in Brooklyn. On January 11, 1918, he was convicted and sentenced to one year and six months in Sing Sing Prison in Ossining, New York. He was later transferred to Auburn Prison, which was then known as the toughest lockup in the New York State correctional system. Lepke was released on January 27, 1919, and again returned to his Lower East Side haunts.

On April 23, 1919, Buchalter was arrested in Manhattan on another burglary charge, which was later thrown out by a magistrate. By this time, many Lower East Side gang leaders were taking notice of this young, but unsuccessful loft burglar. On January 21, 1920, Lepke was arrested again and charged with burglary. Out on bail, he was arrested as a burglary suspect on February 26, 1920, and released. In June 1920, Buchalter was convicted of burglary third degree and sentenced to eighteen months in state prison. Released on parole March 6, 1922, Lepke walked out of Sing Sing Prison and into the Jazz Age.

U.S. Prohibition had begun at midnight January 16, 1920, and the Noble Experiment was entering its third year. Once Lepke was released from his second bit in state prison, he began to appreciate that the loner in the underworld had none of the protection and opportunity afforded those who ran with a gang. From the time Lepke left prison in 1922 until he slammed into his final series of legal problems in 1939 and 1940, he always moved with a gang. He would be arrested eleven more times between 1922 and 1939 for everything from assault to homicide and never saw the inside of a jail.[20]

According to one scholar, the new atmosphere of

national Prohibition recommitted Italian and Jewish criminals to criminality by the variety of rewards. Prohibition broke down the fragile distinction between the legitimate and illegitimate. There was a rebirth of old-fashioned street gangsterism in the form of extortion, racketeering, gambling, and drug dealing, as well as in the rich black market of alcohol.[21]

When Lepke returned to New York City in 1922, he rejoined his old comrade in arms, Jacob Shapiro. Shapiro was working as a labor slugger for "Little Augie" Orgen's mob of strong-arm men. Buchalter also went to work for Orgen as a labor slugger and found his niche as a labor racketeer in the Lower East Side underworld. Labor racketeering had been evolving since the late nineteenth century in the New York City garment industry and paralleled the rise of the needle-trade unions.

There is little doubt that Buchalter and Shapiro worked occasionally as hired sluggers before 1920, but it was during Lepke's apprenticeship to Little Augie that he saw the possibilities of entire industries held captive by, and paying tribute to, gangsters in return for protection. This position of power could be gained through the use of gangster-controlled unions and trade associations. In order to understand Lepke and Gurrah's place as innovators in twentieth-century labor racketeering, it is necessary to look at the origins of the New York underworld's penetration of the garment industry.

2 A Buck a Fist

"Oh, there ain't nothin' to it, I gets my 50, then I goes out and finds the guy they wanna have slugged. I goes up to 'im and I says to 'im, my friend, by way of meaning no harm—and then I gives it to 'im biff in the mug."[1]
—Interview with a labor slugger, 1930

The New York underworld thugs were first employed as labor sluggers during the late nineteenth century when garment-industry employers were attempting to prevent workers in the needle trades from organizing. By the early part of the twentieth century, Lower East Side gang members regularly hired themselves out to both unions and employers in labor disputes.

A Definition of Labor Racketeering

The modern origins of the word "racket" can be traced to the dances thrown by ward politicians in the large eastern cities during the late-nineteenth and early-twentieth centuries. The purpose of these balls was to generate campaign money. The purchase of a quota of tickets to these affairs was expected of the local neighborhood business-people. Nonparticipants could expect legal and other problems. The term racket was probably a slang expression to describe the noise generated by these gatherings.[2]

The same types of rackets were also employed by local gangs as a method of generating income.[3]

By the early twenties, the term racketeer as it applied to the underworld referred to a person who operated an illegal business or service. Racketeering meant crime as an organized means of livelihood.[4]

Racketeering as it evolved in the New York City needle trades and other aspects of the garment industry during the early twentieth century was "the art of levying and collecting tribute by violence and intimidation." The disorganized structure of the small marketplace characteristic of the ethnic economy of New York City's Lower East Side in the early twentieth century facilitated the entry of the underworld into the garment industry for a number of reasons. Prior to 1920, the garment industry was decentralized. Competition was keen, and labor problems were a continual worry for manufacturers. This made the garment industry a perfect target for labor racketeers.[5]

During the early 1900s, incessant labor warfare marked the New York garment industry. Garment manufacturers had decentralized their plants with the massive wave of immigration into the United States in the 1880s. With cheap labor provided by mostly eastern European Jews, garment manufacturers began to assemble clothing by the use of piecework. Sweatshops were often operated in tenement apartments and loft buildings. By this system, manufacturers no longer had to maintain large plants and risk the uncertainties of a boom-or-bust business.

Workers in the garment industry labored under deplorable conditions, sometimes fifteen hours a day, seven days a week. No provisions were made for their health or safety. As a result of these conditions, labor frequently rebelled. Picket lines were set up by the fledgling garment-industry unions. Employers would hire thugs to beat up the pickets, and the unions would hire thugs to prevent strikebreakers from entering shops and to administer beatings to their bosses. This situation offered an excellent opportunity for East Side gangs adept at the use of violence to sell their services to the highest bidder.[6]

The New York needle-trade unions and other trade organizations sought the use of gangsters during the late nineteenth century for several reasons. Hired thugs were used by union leaders for defensive purposes, such as the protection of workers against the antiunion practices of employers. Gangsters were employed to organize workers and in some cases, to terrorize union members suspected of disloyalty. Union leaders sometimes resorted to gangsters to further their own careers and to line their pockets through kickbacks and sweetheart contracts.[7]

Once the garment-industry unions were effectively infiltrated by the underworld, employers were often tempted into a corrupt relationship with trade unions for several reasons. First, they might hope that through a bribe to union officers, they could be persuaded not to organize their shops, allowing for payment of a less-than-going union wage. Such an arrangement was particularly beneficial when the competitors were organized. Second, if union organization could not be prevented, a lenient sweetheart contract could be arranged for a fee. Third, even if an employer could not stop effective organization of his work force, the union itself might be used for the benefit of the employer through the limitation of competition. Competition could be limited by the employer either through the refusal to work on goods or by directly enforcing price agreements.[8] Lower East Side gang leader Monk Eastman became the first modern-era underworld character to turn a profit from labor strong-arm work.

The Monk Eastman Gang Became the First Organized Labor Sluggers

Monk Eastman, born Edward Osterman (1873–1920), became the first Lower East Side gang leader to be involved in labor related strong-arm work. As early as 1897, Eastman provided thugs for hire in labor disputes.[9] The Eastman gang and the Five Points gang of the same period could be considered the first underworld organizations to resemble what we know as modern organized-crime groups. Both these organizations of criminals operated under the political protection of Tammany Hall. Under Monk Eastman's rule, the Eastman gang forced thieves, gamblers, and brothel operators to pay it a regular fee for protection. He also furnished gangs of strong-arm men for hire to employers for assaulting "scabs" and to individuals to resolve private grievances.[10]

The garment industry first used Lower East Side gangs to solve a labor disorder in 1897 when some radicals incited a handful of garment workers to ask for a pay increase. One employer answered these demands by calling on Eastman, who led a group of thugs into an attic workroom on Allen Street. Eastman and his toughs beat up two men who were reported to be union organizers. Although the Eastman gang gained the infamous reputation of being the first labor sluggers in the garment industry, the unimaginative Eastman failed to see labor racketeering as a continuing source of income.[11]

Eastman started a tradition of breaking strikes known

among gangsters as "schlamming," which was later used by loan sharks on delinquent borrowers. All this method required was a length of lead pipe wrapped in a newspaper. This became the weapon of choice among strong-arm thugs. In the coming years as the garment industry was rocked by strikes, labor slugging became a way for even the most down-on-his-luck underworld character to make a living as a schlammer.[12]

In 1904, Monk Eastman was convicted of assault in the first degree and sentenced to ten years in Sing Sing Prison.[13] The original charge of felonious assault had grown out of a scuffle that Eastman and an associate had gotten into when they tried to rob a man whose family had hired a Pinkerton detective to act as a bodyguard. When the Pinkerton agent chased Eastman, the gangster fired several rounds at the detective and ran right into the arms of a policeman, who promptly knocked Eastman unconscious with his nightstick.[14]

Although Monk Eastman merely dabbled in labor slugging, he left behind a legacy for former Eastman gangsters. This was to lay the foundation for twentieth-century labor racketeering in the New York City needle trades. Some of Eastman's closest aides would become the premier labor racketeers of the early twentieth century. It was out of this dynasty of former Eastman associates that the first widely known Lower East Side underworld character became involved in one of the first modern labor disputes in the New York garment industry. Big Jack Zelig, born William Alberts (1882–1912), had been an Eastman lieutenant. He assumed the mantle of leadership over the remains of the old Eastman mob after the murder of Monk's successor, Max Zwiebach, in 1908.[15]

The Era of Big Jack Zelig and Dopey Benny Fein

Once Big Jack Zelig became the leader of the Eastman gang, he expanded its scope of operations and even set up a price list for strong-arm services.

Slash on cheek with knife:	$1–$10
Shot in leg:	$1–$25
Shot in arm:	$5–$25
Throwing a bomb:	$5–$50
Murder:	$10–$100[16]

It was only natural for Zelig, who had much-better organizational skills than Eastman, to see the possibilities of labor racketeering in the garment industry. The opportunity for Zelig and his henchmen came during the first major strike in the garment industry.

The garment industry grew rapidly during the early years of the twentieth century. The thousands of laborers in all facets of the clothing industry, including workers in women's and men's apparel, furs, and hats, were becoming increasingly militant toward employers. In the industry's rank and file of workers, a new crop of class-conscious men and women, many of them former members of the Polish and Austrian socialist and trade-union movements, were providing more-able leadership. Garment workers began to organize and protest against the intolerable working conditions of the period. In 1909, 20,000 female shirtwaist workers struck the industry and stayed out for six months.[17]

Among the first Lower East Side gangsters to be hired as schlammers by the unions during the shirtwaist workers strike were Big Jack Zelig; another former Eastman gangster named Joseph Rosenweig, aka "Joe the Greaser";

and a Lower East Side gang leader named Pincus "Pinchy" Paul. When the strike was over, Zelig stayed on as an organizer for two needle-trade unions.[18] Zelig held this position until he was murdered.

On the evening of October 5, 1912, Zelig left an East Side café and stepped onto a Second Avenue streetcar at Fifth Avenue. At the next stop, an underworld character known as Phil "Red" Davidson hopped aboard. Just before the car reached Fourteenth Street, Davidson walked up behind Zelig and killed him with a single shot through the head.[19]

It was under the tutelage of Big Jack Zelig that the first modern labor racketeer emerged in the person of Benjamin "Dopey Benny" Fein. Fein had been a lesser-known Eastman gangster who gained a reputation as a "shtarker" or strong-arm man during the shirtwaist workers strike in 1909 and the Great Cloakmakers' Strike of 1910. In the aftermath of the Cloakmakers' strike, Jewish civic and labor leaders drew up a document known as the Protocols of Peace. This contract established a fifty-hour workweek, the preferential open shop, and abolished inside subcontracting in the garment industry. Although the protocols represented a major victory for garment-center labor, it was not nearly as recognized and respected by employers as the framers might have wished.[20]

Many needle-trade unions decided to keep on the hired schlammers that had made their cause successful during the labor strife. As a result, in the aftermath of the Cloakmakers' strike, Dopey Benny and his gang became an integral part of the Lower East Side labor movement. For four years, Fein and his henchmen were on the payroll of the United Hebrew Trades (UHT).[21]

Dopey Benny was born Benjamin Fein on the Lower East Side in 1889. As a youngster, Fein quickly became a prodigy of the streets, working as a pickpocket and thief. It was during his childhood that Fein gained the nickname "Dopey Benny" due to his heavy eyelids, which gave him a sleepy look. In reality, there was nothing dopey about Benjamin Fein. His peculiar appearance was the result of an adenoid condition.[22]

As a young man, Fein served several successive terms in Elmira Reformatory and Sing Sing Prison for various offenses including armed robbery. In 1910 after having just been released from a three-year stretch in prison, Fein joined Big Jack Zelig's gang and immediately found himself involved in the growing conflict between the unions and manufacturers in the garment industry.[23] It was during this time that Fein left his previous occupations of pickpocketing and rolling drunks for labor racketeering. Fein shrewdly took advantage of the unsettled conditions following the Great Cloakmakers' Strike of 1910.

Before the turn of the twentieth century, unions often used their own membership, particularly those endowed with brawn, to do the dirty work of physical intimidation. Eventually, professional gangsters replaced the volunteers, for their methods were both less dangerous and far more effective than those employed by strong-arm union men. Although Monk Eastman was one of the first Lower East Side gang leaders to use his fists on behalf of the infant needle-trades union movement, Dopey Benny institutionalized the practice. Fein's methods were once described by a journalist as medieval, but conducted under modern conditions. According to this account, "personally, he so seems to have done his work like an artist and although he did not like to throw any woman down a cellar, when that painful task fell to his lot he did not shirk his duty."[24]

Fein built up a strong organization of gunmen and by the early teens was drawing a fat income by hiring his men out to various factions in the strikes that were so common on the Lower East Side then.[25] During his four-year association with the United Hebrew Trades, the Dopey Benny Fein mob was contracted to do the gorilla work.[26] Almost every strike on the Lower East Side occurred under the auspices of the UHT.

Fein and his men were placed on the payroll of various needle-trade unions on an annual basis or for the duration of a strike. Fein's men were then given pink sheets and union cards as pickets or union delegates. The pink sheet was a four-by-six-inch sheet of paper that was signed by the general strike committee of the International Ladies Garment Workers Union (ILGWU). The pink sheet allowed Fein and his men to pose as pickets in a particular strike and enabled them to walk the street with the regular pickets. Dopey's gang used bats, clubs, blackjacks, and on rare occasions, guns. By masquerading as pickets, Fein and his men protected striking workers from physical attack by management thugs.

At other times, Dopey Benny's gang was hired to destroy shops and beat certain people.[27] On one occasion, Fein hired a gang of female thugs to make raids on factories that employed only women, where men would have difficulty obtaining access. The business of the women was to wreck the shops where employers had not complied with all of the demands of the union. Armed with hairpins and umbrellas weighted with lead slugs, they were very effective.[28] It was not uncommon for Dopey

Benny's mob to stab and slug for unions in one district and against them in another.[29]

During the four-year period that the Dopey Benny gang was employed by the United Hebrew Trades, there was scarcely a strike in the garment industry or ragpickers, sign printers, and umbrella makers in which the Fein gang did not play a part. During this time, Dopey Benny's personal income averaged between $15,000 and $20,000 a year as a labor racketeer. His gang was so widely feared that a group of employers once offered him $15,000 if he would remain neutral during a threatened strike. Fein reportedly refused, saying that his heart was with the working man.[30]

For his services, Fein charged between $25 and $50 a week and an additional $10 a day for each of his men, of which he pocketed $2. He also had a schedule of prices for different tasks similar to the price list composed by Big Jack Zelig. Shooting a scab or guard in the leg cost the union $50, breaking an arm $200, and murder as much as $500 per victim.[31]

Dopey Benny not only had standards, he was an astute businessman who sought to control competition from rival gangs by forming alliances with them. For several years, Fein enjoyed a virtual monopoly on labor racketeering. He divided the city into districts and parceled out strike work on the basis of geography. If a labor union called a strike on the Upper West Side, the territory of the Hudson Dusters Gang, the Hudson Dusters had exclusive rights to it.[32]

As was the case with many Lower East Side gangs, labor slugging was only a sideline of the Hudson Dusters, whose specialty was robbing piers and warehouses. It was conservatively estimated that the Dusters were stealing approximately $1,250,000 worth of goods a year.[33]

If a strike were called on the Lower East Side, only Dopey Benny's mob could lay claim to it. Fein not only rationalized the business of labor racketeering, but by these methods, broadened his base of operations as well. Although firmly rooted in the Jewish ethnic economy, Fein enlisted the cooperation and friendship of gangs throughout the city.[34]

In the fall of 1914, police caught Fein threatening to kill a disgruntled business agent of the butchers union named B. Zalmanowitz. A year earlier, Zalmanowitz had contracted with Fein to protect striking butchers. The job had not been performed to Zalmanowitz's satisfaction, and he refused to pay Fein his $600 fee. Terrorized by Dopey Benny, the frightened business agent called police. Detectives stood by and watched one September day as Dopey Benny repeated his threats to Zalmanowitz. Fein was promptly arrested on first-degree extortion charges. Fein expected to be immediately released on bail provided by his union protectors and was shocked when none of his friends came forward with the bail money. By this time, Dopey Benny may have become too much of a liability to the union. Languishing in jail, Fein realized that he had been double-crossed.[35]

Fein's problems were compounded by his ongoing war with the Five Points gang led by Jack Sirocco. The Five Pointers refused to cooperate with the Dopey Benny Fein mob in an alliance for racketeering rights on the Lower East Side. In late 1914, another Lower East Side gang leader and former Eastman thug, Joseph Rosenweig, aka "Joe the Greaser," confessed to the murder of labor racketeer Pincus "Pinchy" Paul. He also named Fein as one of a group of men involved in a January 1914 shootout with the Five Points gang in which an innocent pedestrian named Frederick Strauss was accidentally shot and killed. Two members of the Dopey Benny mob were tried for this murder and acquitted.[36]

As a result of these ongoing problems, Fein decided to talk to Manhattan District Attorney Charles Perkins and explain what he knew about the underworld's ties to labor in exchange for leniency in his pending legal problems. His revelations spun an amazing tale several hundred pages long in which Fein described the history of labor racketeering on the Lower East Side.

He named Samuel Liebowitz, president of the United Hebrew Trades, and several ILGWU bosses as the people who gave his gang work. Perkins empaneled a grand jury. After listening to Fein's confessions over a period of three months, in May 1915, Perkins charged twenty-three needles-trade labor leaders and eleven gangsters with extortion, assault, riot, and murder.

The bill of indictment contended that the defendants had conspired to murder Herman Liebowitz. Liebowitz was a cloak maker and member of the Cloakmakers and Suitmakers union. He had taken a job at a nonunion shop in upstate New York during the Cloakmakers' strike of 1910. When he returned to union headquarters in New York City after the strike ended, he was reprimanded and beaten to death on July 31, 1910.[37] Seven garment industry labor leaders were eventually tried for the murder of Liebowitz. These labor bosses were Morris Stumpmaker and Max Sigman, the general secretary and treasurer of the International Ladies Garment Workers

Union; Solomon Metz, president of the United Hebrew Trades; Julius Woolf, general manager of the Cloak and Suitmakers Union; Max Singer, a former member of the board of directors of the Cloak and Suitmakers Union; Isadore Auspitz; and Abraham Neidinger.[38]

The trial of the seven leading trade unionists opened with great publicity on September 24, 1915. The chief defense attorney, Morris Hilquit, realizing he could not win the case by refuting the state's argument point by point, decided to use a technique pioneered by Clarence Darrow. This technique was to place the deed in its social context, explaining how it came about and why the perpetrators should not be found guilty.[39] On October 8, 1915, the seven defendants were found not guilty. The other sixteen labor leaders and gangsters were later released for lack of evidence.[40]

The significance of the trial was that it exposed the intrusion of Lower East Side organized-crime groups into the needle-trade unions. This was the beginning of a permanent presence of organized crime in the New York garment industry. Fein was reported to have gone legitimate after the trials and disappeared from both the public and police record.

It was around this time that a former Dopey Benny mob slugger emerged as a Lower East Side gang boss. This thug's name was Jacob "Little Augie" Orgen. Orgen represented the last of the old-time labor sluggers. It was under the tutelage of Little Augie that Louis "Lepke" Buchalter and Jacob "Gurrah" Shapiro got their start in labor racketeering.

3 Little Augie

"A long trail of cracked skulls and mutilated bodies bespoke the mob's efficiency. Their names spread fear and dread throughout the lower eastside."[1]

Little Augie (1901?–1927) was born Jacob Orgen or Orgenstein in Austria and brought to Manhattan's Lower East Side in the first years of the twentieth century. His parents were respectable people, and his older brothers found employment as legitimate tradesmen in the garment industry. As a youngster, Jacob was attracted to the streets of the Lower East Side. His childhood was not unlike that of other notorious gangsters of the period, like Monk Eastman or "Dopey" Benny Fein. This was the beginning of an era when old-fashioned street thuggery was evolving into modern organized crime. Little Augie represents one of the last of the old-style neighborhood gangsters whose stock in trade was violence.

The name "Little Augie" was actually a corruption of Orgen, and because of his small physical stature, "Little" seemed to fit. Orgen began his criminal career as a child and became an adept pickpocket and package thief. At thirteen, he greatly enhanced his reputation by engaging in a knife fight with a member of the notorious Kid Dropper gang. Orgen was badly slashed from his left ear to his chin in the scuffle, leaving a raised and conspicuous white scar across his face that marked him for the rest of his life. After this encounter, he was always known to carry a pistol.[2]

Once Orgen developed a reputation for violence, he joined the Dopey Benny Fein gang of labor racketeers in the late teens. It was under the tutelage of Fein that Orgen learned the fine points of labor racketeering.[3] Little Augie was to become the last of the old-time labor racketeers, preferring slugging and quick payoffs from employers and unions to the more-sophisticated infiltration of labor unions by future organized crime.[4]

By 1917, Dopey Benny was out of action as the result of his sensational testimony against the underworld. Orgen then formed his own gang of labor sluggers. It was during this period that Orgen's gang, who were known as the "Little Augies," and the gang of Nathan Kaplan, aka "Kid Dropper," became locked in a desperate feud over the rights to labor racketeering on the Lower East Side. The Little Augies included among their members such future underworld luminaries as Louis "Lepke" Buchalter; Irving Wexler, aka Waxey Gordon; Jacob "Gurrah" Shapiro; Hyman "Curly" Holtz; and John T. Nolan, aka Jack "Legs" Diamond.[5]

The rapidly expanding garment industry of the period was suffering from growing pains. Labor and capital were once again finding it difficult to come to an agreement, especially in the post-World War I recession economy. The result was strikes. Someone had to stop the industrial strife. There were no governmental agencies to handle the job. Gangs like Little Augie's and Kid Dropper's stepped into the breach. They would arbitrate the differences between labor and capital. While they had no judicial equipment to legitimately arbitrate disputes, they did have men armed with knives, guns, and clubs ready to enforce decisions handed down by the gang leaders. Labor knew if it had to come to Little Augie or Kid Dropper to win a strike, so did capital. It cost them heavily. Rates ranging from $10,000 to $125,000 per labor dispute, depending on the size of the trouble and the time needed to break a strike, were common.[6]

Kid Dropper

Kid Dropper was born Nathan Kaplan (1895–1923) on the Lower East Side. He had once been a member of the Five Points gang, who were rivals of the Dopey Benny Fein and Monk Eastman mobs before them. Like Little Augie, Kaplan was also an experienced labor slugger. In 1917, Kaplan was released from Sing Sing Prison. He returned to his Lower East Side haunts where he formed his own gang, which he called the "Rough Riders of Jack the Dropper."[7] Kaplan developed his reputation as the result of a feud with another notorious gunman, Joseph Weyler, aka "Johnny Spanish."

In 1911, Weyler was forced to leave New York after accidentally killing an eight-year-old girl in a street shootout with another gangster. When Weyler returned to the city, he discovered that his former girlfriend was dating Kid Dropper. Weyler made no threats against her, but one night, he forced her into a taxi and drove into a marsh near Maspeth, Long Island. There, he backed her up against a tree, pulled a pistol, and fired several shots into her abdomen. The woman was found unconscious several hours later, but in the process had delivered a baby, three of whose fingers were shot away. Weyler was quickly arrested, convicted, and given seven years for assault.[8] Kid Dropper was arrested several months later on a robbery charge. He was later convicted and received a sentence of seven years in Sing Sing.[9]

When Kid Dropper and Weyler were released in 1917, they renewed their old feud, which had actually started when both were members of the old Five Points gang under Paul Kelly (Paolo Vaccarelli). On July 19, 1919, Johnny Spanish was murdered in front of a restaurant at 19 Second Avenue by three gunmen who came up behind him and emptied their pistols into his body. Kid Dropper was quickly arrested and soon discharged because of lack of evidence.[10]

Kaplan reportedly gained his colorful moniker, "Kid Dropper," as a youngster when he was said to have earned his money by knocking down other youngsters as they were bent over sidewalk craps games and running off with their money. According to other stories, Kaplan was called "Kid Dropper" because he was an expert shot with a pistol.[11] Still another version maintained that Kid Dropper, who was short and powerfully built, had the ability to drop an opponent with one blow from his ham-fist.[12]

The Murder of Kid Dropper

Little Augie's mob and the gang of Kid Dropper had been sniping at each other since 1917. In 1923, a Lower East Side strike resulted in a full-blown gang war between the rival mobs.[13] In that year, Little Augie's gang and a smaller outfit led by Solomon Schapiro combined against Kid

Dropper's mob during a labor dispute of wet-wash laundry workers.[14] Kid Dropper often represented employers in labor disputes, while Little Augie was known to work with unions.[15] Both gangs sometimes hired their men out to both sides during a strike.

The Dropper/Augie gang war soon became one of the bloodiest underworld feuds in New York history. Twenty-three murders were attributed to the war in a period of only a few months.[16] Kaplan vowed to exterminate every member of Little Augie's gang. On August 1, 1923, Jacob Shapiro was shot and badly wounded by a gunman firing from a touring car that sped by Shapiro as he was standing in front of 75 Essex Street. In uncharacteristic underworld fashion, Shapiro identified the gunman as Kid Dropper to the police, the idea being that if Dropper were arraigned and brought to court, an assassin could be waiting in the crowd for him. Kaplan was arrested, and on August 28, 1923, he was brought to Essex Market Magistrates Court in Manhattan to be arraigned on assault charges made against him by Jacob Shapiro, a Little Augie lieutenant.

Shapiro, who had previously identified Dropper as one of three men who had shot him, now changed his mind. Shapiro told the judge that it was dark the night of August 1, and he was now certain that Kid Dropper was not the man who shot him. Magistrate Stanley Renaud dismissed the felonious assault charge against Kaplan, and he was released to the custody of police, who were going to immediately take him to a West Side court where he was to be arraigned on violation of the Sullivan Law, which required a permit for carrying and owning a gun. As Dropper left the courthouse, he was protected by fifteen detectives, ten uniformed officers, and two police captains. It was suspected that Little Augie and his men might try to move on Kid Dropper as he was being transported.

With acting-Detective Jesse Joseph at his side and Capt. Cornelius Willemse a few feet behind him, Kaplan emerged from the courthouse.[17] While Kaplan was being arraigned, a great crowd had gathered in the street to catch a glimpse of the infamous gang leader. Detectives noticed Little Augie and one of his gunmen glaring at Dropper from the crowd, but they did not notice Louis Kushner, aka Louis Cohen, a minor member of the Little Augie mob, lurking in a tenement house doorway across the street.[18]

As Kaplan left the courthouse with the police gauntlet, his wife joined him. The entourage walked to a waiting cab, and Dropper's wife said, "Jack, you've beaten all the other cases, and you'll beat this one uptown." She put her arm around his neck and kissed him. Captain Willemse pushed Mrs. Kaplan to one side as they approached the taxi.

Kaplan climbed into the vehicle and sat on the right side of the backseat. His head could just be seen through the rear window of the cab.[19] Captain Willemse and a detective stood beside the door and delayed the departure of the cab while Willemse gave the driver instructions. As Detective Jesse Joseph climbed in and sat next to Dropper, Kushner broke through the crowd at a run and approached the back of the taxi. Standing on his toes, he could see the back of Kaplan's head.

With the rapidity of a snake, Kushner pressed the muzzle of his revolver against the rear-window glass and pulled the trigger. He fired three shots at a downward angle. The first bullet hit Kid Dropper in the back of the head. Kaplan collapsed onto Detective Joseph's chest. A second shot hit the driver behind the ear. Captain Willemse and a group of detectives leaped toward Kushner thinking Detective Joseph had been shot in the scuffle.

Mrs. Kaplan ran to the back of the cab and grappled with Kushner. He threw her to one side and busted out the remaining glass in the cab's rear window, firing a fourth shot that again struck Kaplan's head. Kaplan muttered "Jesse, they got me" and collapsed into unconsciousness. A fifth shot tore the straw hat from Captain Willemse's head as police flung themselves on Kushner and wrenched the revolver from his hand. Kushner offered no further resistance. Pale and with his eyes glittering wildly, he faced the circle of policemen and sighed, "I got him. I'd like a cigarette."[20]

In reality, Lepke and Jacob Shapiro had put Louis Kushner up to the murder of Kid Dropper. Buchalter painted a glowing picture of the important position in gangland that would go to the man who killed Dropper. There was no chance of getting convicted of first-degree murder and going to the electric chair. Hadn't Kid Dropper threatened the extermination of all his enemies? Kushner was told that the most he would get was five years in prison. Kushner was also promised that he would receive $100 a week for every week he was in prison and a like amount for a job that would be waiting for him upon his release. Kushner later received a sentence of twenty years for the murder.[21]

Kid Dropper was buried in Mount Hebron Cemetery in Brooklyn on August 31, 1923. Police kept a crowd of more than three thousand people in check, suspecting a disruption of the ceremony by members of the Little Augie mob. There were no incidents.[22] Orgen and Sammy Weiss, a lieutenant, were arrested the day of the shooting as accessories and later released.[23]

Kushner insisted that the reason he killed the Dropper was that the gang leader had tried to blackmail him for $500 and when the money was not forthcoming, threatened to kill him. He was ably represented by then state Sen. Jimmy Walker, later to become infamous as New York City's most-corrupt mayor during the late twenties. Walker worked out a deal with the prosecutor whereby Kushner was tried on manslaughter charges and received a light sentence for what otherwise could have meant the death penalty. He was murdered in a Buchalter-ordered hit in 1939.[24]

After the murder of Kid Dropper in 1923, Orgen emerged as the kingpin of labor racketeering in the New York underworld. His most able lieutenant, Louis "Lepke" Buchalter, attempted to persuade Orgen to get out of the muscle end of the labor business and instead infiltrate and control the garment-industry unions. Orgen refused to listen, opting instead for the fast buck. Times were rapidly changing, however, and a series of communist-inspired riots and strikes in the garment industry during the midtwenties spelled the beginning of the end for Jacob "Little Augie" Orgen and the rise of Lepke.

The Communist Strikes

By the era of Little Augie and the end of World War I, the deadly conflict between the garment unions and manufacturers seemed to be resolved. Continued prosperity made it easier for employers to recognize the unions as the workers' bargaining agents and grant them comparatively generous concessions in return for the stability the union provided. By 1921, however, wartime prosperity had run its course. The recession of that year brought on new hardships in the garment industry. As profits fell, more and more manufacturers lengthened the workweek, increased production schedules, and restored the old contracting-out system. It appeared that war was once again being declared on the unions. The progress made since the massive labor uprisings of 1907 and 1913 was coming apart.

As the conflict between the garment unions and the manufacturers deepened, gangsters were once again brought in. Exactly which garment-industry faction was responsible for bringing in the underworld has never been determined and remains an academic question.[25]

There were four major components in the garment industry of the early twenties. These were women's clothing, men's clothing, furs, and hats. All of these specialties involved many different types of manufacturing procedures, making the manufacture of a garment a complex process. Cloth was shrunk or stretched depending on the material and purpose intended. Pattern makers cut the cloth according to designers' specifications, and machine operators sewed the pieces together.

The men who formed the needle-trade unions were realists. If employers hired thugs, then unions would have to fight them using similar methods.[26] Complicating matters further, each of the needle-trade unions were divided into two sharply hostile factions, one led by the Communists and the other by the Socialists. Each side accused the other of using gangsters, and both readily employed thugs during the conflict.[27]

By 1925, the garment-industry unions had accumulated a lot of money and had big war chests. Within the needle-trade unions, the restless communist elements had grown into positions of power from which they could dictate policy and call strikes. The communist faction was viewed by observers of the period as having two principal objectives that were unrelated to the betterment of wages and working conditions. These objectives were to gain control of the needle-trade unions and by doing so, create enough trouble and disruption to make converts to the revolutionary cause.[28]

The situation came to a head in 1925 when Max Sigman, president of the International Ladies Garment Workers Union, responded to what he viewed as the threat of a union takeover by suspending all of the communist-dominated locals. The officers of Local 22, considered to be the leading communist local in the ILGWU, were physically evicted from their offices. The gauntlet had been thrown down.

In retaliation, the ousted communist locals set up the Joint Action Committee, which was in effect a rival union, to coordinate left-wing activity in the ILGWU.[29] The communist factions of the ILGWU took the strike of 1925 a step further. That year, in preparation for the predicted upcoming conflict, they sent representatives to see underworld power broker Arnold Rothstein, who at that time was arguably the most-powerful underworld leader in the country. By the midtwenties, Rothstein maintained a flourishing business in New York City supplying gangsters for strong-arm work to the furriers and garment workers unions. For his labor services, Rothstein received fees running into the hundreds of thousands of dollars. The ILGWU was reported to have paid Rothstein thousands of dollars to ensure that the police of two NYPD precincts were paid off so that the Communists could foment trouble in the garment district. Buying the police department by precincts meant that uniformed police and detectives would not break up picket lines. They would maintain a convenient blindness to such street violence that broke out as the result of communist agitation. Rothstein would also put in the fix in the lower city courts so that strikers who were arrested would be quickly released.[30]

The situation was made to order for Little Augie and his men. They happily found themselves in a seller's market. Their services as goons and schlammers commanded a higher and higher price. Not only Little Augie, but John T. Nolan ("Legs Diamond") (1897–1931) offered the services of his gang to anyone in the garment industry who would buy them. Conditions were set for a fresh round of gang warfare with the New York garment-manufacturing district as a battleground. The purge of the communist factions of the ILGWU was least successful from the International's point of view in New York City where the single-largest body of workers was concentrated. In New York, the communists effectively controlled the union's decision-making body.

Resisting Sigman's 1925 purge of communist-dominated locals, the Joint Action Committee set up its own autonomous organization, collecting dues, handing out cards, and bargaining with employers without formally breaking with the International. Meanwhile, the cloak-

and-suit manufacturers, the biggest group in the garment industry, were exploiting the factional conflict in the ILGWU and presenting a hard line to the union. The cloak-and-suit manufacturers took such a firm stance against concessions that the Socialist and Communist workers threatened to go on strike.[31]

Finally, in the summer of 1926, the situation exploded into labor conflict. New York State Gov. Alfred E. Smith intervened in the growing dispute. He appointed a commission to recommend the basis of a fair settlement between the cloak-and-suit manufacturers and the divided ILGWU. In June 1926, the commission handed down its recommendations. The manufacturers reluctantly accepted them, as did the International. The communist Joint Action Committee rejected them as humiliating and called a general strike. The strike affected fifty thousand workers and lasted twenty-six weeks.[32]

It was later reported that the Joint Action Committee spent $3.5 million on the strike, yet it eventually had to throw in the towel and accept the commission's original recommendations. A major gang war nearly erupted during the labor action. The manufacturers were represented by the Legs Diamond mob, whose job was to protect plants and scabs and to terrorize the pickets and union men. Little Augie's gang was hired by the Joint Action Committee to protect the pickets and union cadre.[33] During the strike, Little Augie personally killed a picket named Samuel Landman. He was later tried and acquitted of the shooting.[34] The strike was called off only because the two gathering underworld armies agreed to do so.

When the communist factions who ran the Joint Action Committee sued for peace, they agreed to use

Arnold Rothstein as the mediator.[35] Rothstein agreed to the proposal and quickly persuaded the Legs Diamond gang to stop working for the employers. A telephone call was reported to have solved the problem. Another telephone call took Little Augie's gang out of the picture. Rothstein then got the bosses and the Joint Action Committee together.

It has been theorized that Rothstein saw his role as mediator as a scheme that would allow the underworld to muscle into the garment industry. One writer suggests that Rothstein actually arranged two settlements, one between the Joint Action Committee and bosses, and the other, on which the first rested, between the two rival gangs. Under the terms of this settlement with the underworld, they would all share the spoils and maintain their footholds and steady source of income in the ladies-garment industry. Rothstein in reality was the mediator of gangsters' interests and not those of the unions or manufacturers. Once they were invited in by the employers and unions in a time of conflict, the underworld could not be invited out.[36]

The failure of the communist factions to accomplish their goal in 1926 did not deter them in other areas of the garment industry. In 1927, left-wingers of the International Fur Workers Union pulled a strike in that segment of the industry. Gangsters were brought in to do the same jobs, and the aid of Rothstein was once again sought. By 1927, organized crime was well entrenched in the garment industry.

During this period of labor conflict, Buchalter, Shapiro, and Holtz, Little Augie's most-valuable lieutenants, all tried to persuade Augie to get out of the muscle end of the labor-racketeering business and infiltrate and gain control of key needle-trade unions. Orgen, who was always out for a quick buck, would have none of it. As a result, dissension grew within the ranks of the Little Augie mob.

Buchalter, Shapiro, and Holtz reasoned that instead of settling strikes quickly for a lump-sum payoff, more could be gained by prolonged strikes that increased the chances for everyone to make a profit and opened opportunities to infiltrate unions once the strikes ended. The difference in philosophy among the four allied gangsters came to a head in 1927 over a $50,000 fee that Orgen collected from the Brooklyn Boss Painters Association to end a strike that year.[37]

Augie readily accepted the fee, which he was promptly directed by Buchalter to return. The dispute erupted in deadly violence. Little Augie's approach to the strike was the same as always. Orgen called upon the union leaders and told them that they would all be murdered unless the strike ended immediately. This disagreement over policy created a permanent rift between Orgen and Buchalter. Buchalter and Shapiro became further enraged when Little Augie formed an alliance with Jack "Legs" Diamond and his brother, Eddie. In return for the Diamond brothers' help in ending the Boss Painters strike, Augie split the $50,000 fee with them.[38] Now in fear of his former aides, Orgen hired Legs Diamond as his personal bodyguard.[39]

4 The Gorilla Boys Take Over

"Compared to Lepke, 'Little Augie' was nothing more than the old fashioned neighborhood gangster incarnate."[1]

On the night of October 15, 1927, the Lepke-Gurrah forces were on the prowl for Little Augie. At about 8:00 P.M., Augie was located with his bodyguard, Legs Diamond, on the corner of Norfolk and Delancey streets on Manhattan's Lower East Side. As Buchalter slowly pulled the black touring car to the curb, Shapiro leaped out of the vehicle with a pistol in his hand and began firing. Diamond turned quickly and drew his gun.

Little Augie was killed, and Diamond suffered several bullet wounds including two below the heart. Little Augie was struck once by a bullet in the temple. He was dead before his body hit the ground. Diamond was taken to Bellevue Hospital, where he slowly recovered from his wounds. He was held by police as a material witness.[2] When questioned by detectives, Diamond told them, "Don't ask me nothing, and don't bring anybody here for me to identify. Even if I knew they did it, I wouldn't put the finger on them."[3]

Little Augie was buried at Mount Judah Cemetery in Queens in a massive cherry-red coffin lined with white satin. On the lid gleamed a silver plate: "Jacob Orgen Age 26 Years." It was later claimed that his real age was thirty-three. But it had been eight years since he assumed active leadership of his gang, and on that day, his father had proclaimed him dead.[4]

According to one account, Little Augie was slain because he had double-crossed his partners.[5] Strangely, this was close to the truth. Orgen's passing marked the end of the old-time labor sluggers and the beginning of an era in which the key garment-industry unions would be under the control of organized crime. This situation would evolve once Buchalter and Shapiro infiltrated and took over the existing needle-trade rackets. This would eventually lead to underworld control of a significant sector of the garment industry by the early thirties.

On October 27, 1927, Buchalter and Shapiro turned themselves in to the police. They had been wanted for questioning in the murder of Little Augie. Both men claimed they had attended a movie the night of the murder. They were quickly released for lack of evidence.[6] On November 19, 1927, Hymie "Curly" Holtz was standing on a Bronx street corner with a friend when both men were wounded in a drive-by shooting. Control had been firmly wrested by Lepke and Gurrah, but the attempt on Holtz's life had to be avenged. Louie "Louie the Wop" Fabrizio, an Augie faction hanger-on, had been identified as one of the men who shot at Holtz. He was tracked down and murdered.

Lepke and Gurrah were able to give full play to their earlier ideas. They expanded with the dress industry, whereas Little Augie did not care to what type of business he sent his hoods. The new combination drew a line on the garment trade and its allied industries. Although by doing this they limited themselves in scope, their territory was enlarged to take in the five boroughs of New York City, as well as Massachusetts, Connecticut, and Pennsylvania. They also employed new tactics. Terrorism was not their only weapon. Profit dangled before the nose of a susceptible union leader or trade association proved to be an argument difficult to resist.[7]

The new underworld dynasty on the Lower East Side had a somewhat quieting effect after the murder of Little Augie in 1927. Killings were significantly reduced for a while. Instead of using his sluggers and gunmen to terrorize the needle-trade unions, Lepke worked his men directly into the garment-industry trade organizations. By threat and sometimes violence, the Lepke mob took control of one union local after another. Big labor leaders who were used to having East Side gangsters withdraw from the field after they put down strikes found themselves sharing their leadership with Lepke, Shapiro, and Hymie "Curly" Holtz.[8]

Lepke completely changed the face of labor racketeering in the New York City needle-trade unions. He was methodical in his approach, and as a result, organized crime gained a permanent foothold, not only in the needle-trade unions, but in the entire New York City garment industry. Early in their association, Buchalter and Shapiro won the label of the "Gorilla Boys" for their efficiency in strong-arm work. Later when they raked in millions of dollars a year from the captive garment industry, they became known in the underworld as the "gold dust twins."[9]

Buchalter learned during his years working for Little Augie that the way to take over whole industries was through captive labor unions and captive trade associations. Thus, you had both management and labor in your pocket. Lepke's system for taking control of labor unions was simple. A labor leader would hire Lepke and his mob to beat up union rebels. After the disturbing element in the union ranks was subdued through mayhem and intimidation, Lepke would not only keep his men in the union, but would put his handpicked officers in place to take control of the organization. Lepke's strong-arm men would then remain in the union local. From that point, on all subsequent union elections were Lepke controlled.

Buchalter wedged his way into the garment-center manufacturing concerns in a similar way. Manufacturers would hire Lepke's guns for use as strikebreakers. Soon afterward, the manufacturers would realize that once they did business with Lepke, they were carrying him on their backs.[10] Some observers of the period theorized that some business concerns actually preferred to deal with racketeer-controlled unions. In these situations, the cost of protection was less than the cost of labor when dealing with honest unions. Also, the cost of carrying racketeers on the payroll was offset by paying labor less to make up the difference.[11] Owners who tried to resist the Lepke mob would have their business establishments destroyed, be beaten, murdered, or have acid thrown in their faces. When a plant owner weakened, Lepke would place his own men in the plant.[12] An associate of Buchalter's during the time he worked as a strikebreaker for Little Augie in the early twenties once observed, "Lep loves to hurt people."[13]

By 1929, Lepke employed a force of fifty assorted hoodlums, bookkeepers, and "foremen," the latter assigned as watchdogs in plants where Lepke had reason to distrust the legitimate management. Professional killers started out at $25 a week and progressed, by display of their special skills, to $150.[14]

In 1929, Lepke was involved in the last industrial terrorism job in which he personally had a hand. Early in 1929, a garment-workers union went out on strike, demanding higher wages and a closed shop. A closed shop indicates a plant where only union members are employed. Due to the violence with which Lepke and Gurrah threw themselves into the fray, the strike was nearly won. The manufacturing establishment of M&L Rosenblatt Inc. at 725 Broadway proved to be a tough nut to crack. It resisted Lepke's picket line and threats. Early one morning Lepke, Gurrah, and three other men pried their way into the fifth-floor loft where the shop was located. Armed with steel bars, corroding acids, and stench bombs, they went to work. The steel bars twisted the machinery into useless shapes. The acid burned through $25,000 worth of merchandise. The stench bombs ruined what the acid could not reach. The five men were arrested at the scene and charged with the crime. Witnesses told of having seen them enter the plant. The plant owner detailed their threats.

Unfortunately, as was always the case, when the witnesses finally went to court, they suffered severe memory loss. Threats were forgotten, faces looked different. The three men who were arrested with Lepke and Gurrah were Lou Kravitz, a lieutenant of Lepke's; Irving Gordon; and Philip Silver. These arrests completed the criminal educations of the twin heralds of death and destruction. It was the last time they ever committed an act of violence in person. They had ceased being shtarkers (Yiddish for tough guys) and gorillas. They had become underworld businessmen running their illicit affairs in open defiance of the law.[15]

Lepke's approach to racketeering was unique for its time. While other gangsters concentrated on liquor, loan-sharking, gambling, and prostitution, Lepke set his sights on the necessities of life—clothing, food, and transportation.[16] Lepke's first move as a gang leader was carefully planned.

The strikes of 1925 and 1926 influenced the direction in which he wanted to go with labor racketeering in the New York garment industry. The Amalgamated Clothing Workers led by Sidney Hillman was the parent body of many needle-trade labor unions. This group of skilled workers turned out 15 percent of the men's clothing manufactured in the U.S. The heart of the business was the cutters union. The cutter's job was to cut out sections of a garment from patterns. Membership of the cutters union numbered only 1,800 people. Another eighty were Teamsters employed as truck drivers. They moved the goods from one location and process to another. It was obvious to Lepke that the entire clothing industry rested on a foundation of less than 1,900 workers.[17]

In 1928, Lepke moved in on the cutters union by persuading certain leaders of the organization that it would be to their advantage to take in his entire crew and get rid of the union's two full-time musclemen. Then a Lepke-controlled business agent named Philip Orlovsky was put in as manager of the Cutters Local No. 4 in 1931.[18]

In the later twenties, the nature of the garment industry had changed. No longer were there sweatshop conditions. The industry had moved out of the home and poorly equipped factory into the modern skyscraper. The heaviest concentration was in midtown Manhattan and was roughly bounded by Fourteenth Street on the south, Forty-Second Street on the north, and extended from Fifth Avenue on the east to Ninth Avenue on the west. The annual turnover in the industry had grown to tremendous proportions as a result. Estimates for 1931:

1) Fur only (rabbit and muskrat): 100,000,000
2) Dresses: 500,000,000
3) Cotton wash dresses: 103,300,000
4) Men's clothing: 250,000,000[19]

By 1930, Lepke and Gurrah had put together a gang of 250 handpicked "torpedoes." Rather than criminals forcing themselves on victims, by this time, the use of gangsters was an effort by some businessmen to overcome the insecurity of cutthroat competition that existed in the garment industry, especially after 1929 with the advent of the Great Depression. Manufacturers were turning to underworld elements and inviting their help in dealing with excessive competition or troublesome labor problems. By the early thirties, Lepke and Gurrah would have a virtual monopoly on certain aspects of the food industry, New York trucking, and the garment industry.

5 Assault on the Garment Industry and Other Legitimate Businesses

"A rat will find somewhere an opening through which he can enter a house. It is certain the rats of the underworld have found ways to crawl through the meshes of the law and carry on their slimy business in spite of our ardent desire to stop them."[1]

By the late twenties, Buchalter and Shapiro were rapidly gaining control of the men's suits portion of the New York garment industry. They were quick to realize the strategic importance of the cutters union and the pivotal role garment trucking played in the process of completing a suit of clothes. The garment industry operated under the jobber-contractor system. This type of arrangement was particularly vulnerable to gangster influence. Under this system of inside production with workers of all degrees of skill under the same roof, the superior economic power of the highly skilled worker can be used to help unionize the entire plant, so long as the relatively small number of skilled workers refuse to work under nonunion conditions. The plant then can scarcely operate whether or not it enjoys the protection of gangsters.

Under the contracting system, however, the cutters, comprising a large percentage of the skilled workers, may work in the jobbers shop under union conditions. If the cut goods can be sent to nonunion contracting shops within 100 miles or even more, the enterprise can undersell its completely unionized competition. The function of the gangsters is to protect the trucks that haul the cut goods to the contractor and bring the finished product back. Protection of trucking at or near the jobber's office is more important than safeguarding the contracting shop against union organizers.[2]

The two points of control are the cutting room and trucking. When the union is functioning properly, it checks the volume of goods cut with the volume received by inside and authorized contract shops and learns from the truckers where the balance is being taken. If some of the cutters can be persuaded to send false figures to the union office, however, receiving part of the net savings as their share of the loot, and if, in addition, the police and politicians are bought off so that gangsters riding the trucks are not molested in the performance of their duties, then, indeed, the business that receives gangster protection will prosper, and union tailors and legitimate employers will suffer.[3] This was exactly the situation that existed in the New York men's clothing business in the late twenties.

Clothing was a high-risk industry in the 1920s. As styles changed, manufacturers needed ready capital to invest in new materials. Smaller companies often had trouble obtaining bank loans to finance the changes and turned to mobsters for funds. Unable to keep up with exorbitant interest rates, some owners found themselves in business with Lepke and Gurrah.[4]

Buchalter and Shapiro gained control of Local 4 of the cutters union in the late twenties by persuading certain union officials that it would be advantageous if their mob replaced the services of Terry Burns and Abe Slabow, who were at that time Local 4's enforcers. Philip Orlovsky, who had been a Local 4 business agent, became business manager in 1931. Orlovsky was completely controlled by Buchalter.[5] A year or two later, the Amalgamated Clothing Workers Union was rocked by a dispute between the Sidney Hillman group and the Orlovsky faction of the cutters union. In the battle between Hillman and Orlovsky, Buchalter used Orlovsky as a pawn, trading him off for a deal with Hillman. This move was followed by the designation of Bruno Belea, the general organizer of the Amalgamated, and of two Buchalter hoods, Paul Berger and Danny Fields, as the new intermediaries between Buchalter and the union. Later, another of Buchalter's men received $25,000 from Hillman himself for delivery to Buchalter for consummating the deal.

With his position concerning the Amalgamated Clothing Workers secured, Buchalter next turned to management. He extorted anywhere from $5,000 to $50,000 from truckers and individual manufacturers. One of Lepke's most-important operatives, Max Rubin, stated in later trial testimony that from 1934 to 1937, he personally took part in these shakedowns, which for Rubin were from $400 to $700 a week, and he stated that he was only one of many collectors.[6]

According to one scholar, Sidney Hillman was a Congress of Industrial Organizations (CIO) leader with deep criminal ties to the underworld. As president of the Amalgamated Clothing Workers of America, Hillman regularly used the services of Lepke Buchalter. That was Hillman's secret life. In public, he would become known as President Franklin Delano Roosevelt's most-influential adviser, a key administrator of the NRA (National [Industrial] Recovery Act) and later the wartime Office of Production and Management. Inevitably, Lepke collided with Hillman's local in his move to take over key unions in the garment industry. On the record, Hillman struck bold postures against what he called "the curse of under-worldism." But it was just smoke and verbiage, a fine-sounding diversion.[7]

A few years later, when Special Prosecutor Thomas E. Dewey started pursuing labor rackets, he invited Hillman and David Dubinsky of the ILGWU to his home for dinner. "They both dealt with these gangsters and knew all about them," Dewey recalled many years later, "but they wouldn't give me the slightest bit of help of any kind, and they never did. . . . We had to make our own tough way."[8]

Hillman's dealings with Lepke proceeded through stages from resistance to détente to criminal cooperation. At first, Hillman was reported to have attempted to have Lepke and his partner, Gurrah Shapiro, killed, but the job was botched.

For payoffs, Lepke's mob performed various types of muscle work for Hillman. According to subsequent secret testimony of Albert Tannenbaum, a Lepke gangster, Tannenbaum did slugging work on occasion for Hillman. Tannenbaum said when Hillman experienced trouble in connection with the Amalgamated, he would tell Danny Fields or Murray Weinstein (Lepke stooges), and they would transmit the matter to Lepke.[9]

Control of the truckers in the men's clothing business was also necessary to maintain a tight grip on certain aspects of the New York garment industry. This was done cautiously through the use of work stoppages. As explained by a Lepke lieutenant, "When union officials are not sure of getting people out for a strike, they call a stoppage. If it falls down there is nothing said. If it picks up force and people respond, they call it a strike."[10]

Canny gangsters like Lepke and Gurrah recognized the value of the trucking business and, then as now, how easy it was to infiltrate. Because many Teamsters were independent and self-employed, they were susceptible to pressure. The solitary nature of their work left drivers more vulnerable to intimidation than workers in shops. In the garment industry during the twenties and thirties, clothing was not produced in one plant. Unfinished goods were trucked between manufacturers and subcontractors. By blocking transportation, racketeers could bring the whole industry to a halt.[11]

Buchalter accomplished his preeminence in the garment industry by participating in the organization of garment-truck owners and self-employed drivers into an employers trade association, a significant act in the development of business racketeering. One of the first actions of the association was to raise the cartage costs for men's clothing followed by members of the association sharing the windfall profits.[12] To make their point perfectly clear, Buchalter, Shapiro, and other union organizers called a work stoppage through the Amalgamated to prevent garment work from being trucked to nonunion shops primarily in Pennsylvania.

One of the major garment-trucking firms balked at the ordered work stoppage. Buchalter countered the argument by assuring the boss of the company, Louis Cooper, who owned Garfield Express in Passaic, New Jersey, that he had nothing to worry about. Buchalter told Cooper that he (Lepke) was now the Amalgamated. Cooper responded that he would only agree to stop his trucks if Buchalter became his partner. Buchalter agreed, and the trucks stopped.[13] With Lepke as a partner, the Garfield Express Company gained a virtual monopoly over the extensive traffic in garment trucking between New York and New Jersey.[14] Lepke's control of garment trucking by the midthirties was absolute.

In 1935, Max Rubin, a Lepke lieutenant and officer of Teamsters Local 240 of the Amalgamated, took some delivery business away from Morris Blustein, a garment trucker, and gave it to a trucker tied to Lepke. Trying to fight back after getting nowhere with Rubin, Blustein went to see Sidney Hillman. Hillman brushed him off. According to Blustein, "I grabbed him [Hillman] and said, 'You are taking away my bread.' I said, 'Listen, Mr. Hillman, I know that your hands are full of blood. You've killed plenty of people. I'll be damned if you're going to kill me. I need a living. That's all I know. I know that as president of the Amalgamated and anybody that's sitting on the central committee, it's you people that control, that control board, and you people are routing out my work.' He said, 'I've got nothing to do with it, go and see Max Rubin.'"[15]

Refusal to follow the orders of the Buchalter mob had dire consequences. Truckers were beaten or murdered. Truck engines were destroyed by putting emery into the gas tanks. In the end, those trucking companies that had not been put out of business by the Lepke mob submitted completely.

The Fur Industry

The onset of the Great Depression in 1929 created a unique problem in the fur industry. During the boom period of the late twenties, fierce competition could be tolerated. The Depression caused a collapse in the demand for fur. The fur industry was both demoralized and extremely competitive. Because fur manufacturing was a skilled trade, resistant to mechanization and performed largely by hand, access into the industry was simple. The majority of firms were small. About 25 percent had only one or two employees, and more than half employed four workers or fewer. In addition, the fur trade was highly susceptible to fashion changes and quite unstable in prices. The Depression struck the fur industry harder than any of the other needle trades with fur imports dropping by 1932 to one-quarter and exports to one-third the 1929 base. Employers in the fur industry were notoriously uncooperative in facing common industry problems.

Prodded by desperate competition after three years of the Great Depression, the fur dressers invented two organizations they hoped would promote stability and profit. Formed in 1932 were the Protective Fur Dressers Corporation (Protective) consisting of seventeen of the largest rabbit skin-dressing companies in the country, and the Fur Dressers Factor Corporation (Factor), which included forty-six of the largest dressers in fur other than rabbit skins. The purpose and function of both organizations was to eliminate from the industry all the dressing firms that were not members. To persuade all dealers to work only with firms that belonged to the corporations and/or to prevent them from dealing with nonmembers, they would set prices and implement quota systems.

Once the organizations were in place, all the fur dealers and manufacturers were notified that henceforth their business was to be given to a firm designated by the association. They were also told that prices would be increased immediately and all accounts were to be settled in full every Friday.

Samuel Mittelman, a legitimate fur merchant, was selected to be the front man for the protectives. Papers for the organizations were drawn up, and the seal of incorporation was issued by the secretary of state of New York to the Protective Fur Dressers and Factor corporations. The aims of the organizations seemed admirable. According to the prospectus, they would stabilize the fur industry and eliminate labor troubles through collective dealings with the union. Cutthroat competition would be eliminated by fixing prices and imposing penalties on those who violated the price agreements. There was to be a central collection agency for all debts.

On the surface, the protectives sought an admirable goal, but the manufacturers saw behind the glowing front the hand of Lepke. Only 20 percent of the fur manufacturers joined at first. Lepke expected this and visited Morris Langer, president of the Needle Trade Workers Union. He showed Langer how wages could be doubled. In addition to this, if the union threw its support behind the Protective, the latter organization would milk its members' unemployment fund of $250,000 payable annually to the union. A citywide strike was then called, and the fur industry was paralyzed. In the end, the employers gave in. An additional 60 percent of the merchants capitulated. On the recalcitrant 20 percent, Lepke now turned to violence.[16]

The F.B.I. estimated that the Protective controlled 80 to 90 percent of the trade in 1932 and about 50 percent the following year. Those dealers and manufacturers who refused to cooperate with the Protective and continued doing business with independent fur dressers were subject to telephone warnings, beatings, and destruction of their goods by corrosive acids and stench bombs. In extreme cases, some firms were asked to be closed and blown up if they didn't.[17]

Buchalter and Shapiro were brought into the fur industry through the efforts of Abraham Beckerman, previously a high official in the Amalgamated and subsequently general manager of the Fur Dressers Factor Corporation. Beckerman had organizational problems with Factor and solicited the help of Buchalter and Shapiro. It would be the Lepke mob's duty to police and maintain the integrity of this cartel.

As always, the price of using Lepke's people was high. Lepke demanded a kickback of two cents per skin and a straight fee from each member. Prices rose as Lepke consolidated his power. Payments to the Lepke mob were made weekly or shops were bombed, workers beaten, and acid thrown.[18] Julius Bernfield, a partner in Brickman and Denfield, the largest fur-dressing firm in New York, was burned so badly by acid that he lost an eye before deciding to do business with the Protective Fur Dressers Association in 1932.[19]

Bernfield later testified in court, "Three times I was attacked after the Protective Fur Dressers Association demanded that we must turn our business over to them. The first time they threw acid at me while I was driving with my thirteen-year-old daughter. Some of the acid burned her clothes. I complained to Samuel Mittelman, president of the Protective, that it was a terrible thing, not only to attack me but to endanger my daughter's life. He said, 'Best you should turn over your work to us so you won't have any more trouble.' We turned some work over to them, but it wasn't enough. The third time I was attacked, they threw a whole gallon of acid in my face. I was in the hospital for three months. I was home another three months. I can never see out of that eye again."[20]

Lepke's mob was used by both the Protective and the Factor organizations. The Factor had first contracted with a gangster named Jerry Sullivan, a member of the Owney Madden mob, to do the enforcement work. Sullivan's services were unsatisfactory, and the organizations turned to Lepke.

Both workers and manufacturers profited by the stabilization of the fur industry brought about by the organization of the protectives. Once the fur industry was brought in line, however, the protectives took a firmer stance against the unions as the Depression deepened. Backed by Lepke and his mob, the protectives refused to honor commitments given in previous union contracts.[21]

The fact that the Lepke mob was behind the fur manufacturers' attempt to not honor past contracts created problems. The Fur Workers Union was extremely hostile toward the Protective Fur Dressers Association, and Lepke stooges were sent to placate workers and gain a foothold in the Fur Workers Union.

One company was giving the Lepke mob particular trouble, the Acme Fur Tanning Company of Gloversville, New York. When arguments got nowhere, a bomb was thrown into the plant. Still the company refused to join the protective. Lepke sought out Morris Langer, president of the Needle Trade Workers Union, and ordered him to call the workers of the Gloversville Plant out on strike. Langer protested that he couldn't do it. Workers in the plant were receiving union-scale wages, worked short hours, and were extremely happy with conditions in the plant.

"My word is enough reason," Lepke said. Langer protested that he would do anything for Lepke, but this request was an impossibility. "I realize that I asked a lot," Lepke said, patting Langer on the back. "Maybe it's just as well we drop the matter." Langer let Lepke's pleasant smile and affable manner lull his suspicions. It was a fatal error. One week later, March 21, 1933, Langer started his car and was blown to bits by a bomb.[22]

Another furrier, Albert Williams, in later trial testimony, told how his firm initially refused to join the Fur Dressers Factor Corporation. Williams said his first warning was a knife attack that scarred his face from chin to ear. Then he was attacked by a man who beat him with a milk bottle. He was later assaulted by two men armed with a blackjack and an iron pipe.[23]

Lepke's man in charge of strong-arm work in the early days was Harry "Big Greenie" Greenberg. All orders for raids, beatings, bombings, and assassinations had to be transmitted through Big Greenie. Greenberg was born in Yezneirzany, Galacia. Arriving in the United States in 1910, he moved to the Lower East Side where he became acquainted with Lepke and Gurrah. In 1923, Greenberg was deported because of his criminal record, having served a sentence in Sing Sing for safe burglary. He reentered the U.S. illegally. He was arrested, and after losing a deportation hearing, he was released on bail pending appeal. Greenberg jumped his bail and went to work for Lepke as his chief enforcement officer.[24]

The Fur Workers Union was determined to keep Lepke and his mob out of their organization. When the mob pushed, they pushed back. As a result, Buchalter and Shapiro had a great deal of trouble dealing with the fur workers unions. This would eventually lead to the Lepke mob's sudden exit from the fur industry.

Tensions finally reached a climax on April 24, 1933. Lepke mob thugs staged an attack on the headquarters of the Fur Workers Union in Manhattan where a meeting was in progress. Although Lepke's strong-arm men were heavily armed, they met with fierce resistance and were driven out into the street by irate workers. Those workers were joined by others as news of the attack spread throughout the fur district. A number of men were killed and several gangsters were severely beaten. Seven men were later convicted of felonious assault.

This battle effectively ended Lepke's activities in the New York fur industry.[25] It was later claimed that the raid was the direct result of Lepke's failure to force the Gloversville fur plant to shut down. Buchalter was trying to make a point to the Fur Workers Union, but failed to intimidate the workers.

In later trial testimony, it was discovered that the attack had been well planned. A Dannemora prisoner named Sam "Chowderhead" Cohen testified that the day of the raid on the Fur Workers Union, Harry "Big Greenie" Greenberg called him and asked Cohen to meet him at a room in the Arlington Hotel in Manhattan.

"I want you to do me a favor and help break up a

meeting," Cohen quoted Greenberg as saying. He then handed Cohen a piece of iron pipe wrapped in a newspaper. Cohen at the time was a widely known freelance labor slugger. Two men would later die from their wounds in the union office raid.[26]

In November 1933, 158 people were named in three federal indictments charging them with fur racketeering through alleged threats, assaults, hijacking, acid throwing, and bombings. Named in the indictments were seventy-eight individuals and eighty business firms said to control $170 million of business annually. All indictments were based on alleged violations of the Sherman Antitrust Act. The first indictment named the Fur Dressers Factor Corporation. The second was against dealers in rabbit skins. The third listed defendants in the Needle Trades Workers Industrial Union. Louis Buchalter and Jacob Shapiro were two of the names listed in the indictment. It would be almost three years before the two labor racketeers would be brought to justice on the charges. These indictments were the beginning of the end for Buchalter and Shapiro.[27]

Lepke's withdrawal from the fur industry had little effect on his pocketbook. In the early thirties, Buchalter and Shapiro became businessmen and entrepreneurs. In 1933, Joseph Miller, the owner of a New York coat-front manufacturing firm known as the Perfection Coat Front Company, took the two gangsters into the business as one-third partners after Lepke and Gurrah invested $20,000 each. During that period, every suit of men's clothing had a canvas coat front under the material of the coat to make the garment wrinkle free. The Perfection Coat Front Company gave an advantage to Lepke and

Gurrah that went far beyond mere profit. It enabled them to file ostensibly legitimate income-tax returns. Most importantly, it enabled the two gangsters to use the firm as a banking vehicle through which they could funnel checks they received from the mob.[28]

In 1934, Miller sold the Perfection Coat Front plant to Samuel Weiner and moved his operation to Philadelphia. It was only then that Weiner sadly discovered that Buchalter and Shapiro were stockholders in the company. They demanded that Weiner place them on his payroll, stating even though Miller had left New York under an agreement not to open again in the city or sell to his old customers, he would not keep his agreement. Then Weiner would need the services of Lepke and his mob. Buchalter and Shapiro, without any further investment of capital, were taken into the company by Weiner and put on the payroll for $300 a week each. Not satisfied with the salaries paid to them by Weiner, they took additional money from the Perfection Coat Front Company in the form of loans. This resulted in losses to the company of $75,000 from April 12 to September 1, 1934. The company could not obtain additional credit to operate unless Joseph Miller returned to New York to take over its management.

This was yet-another example of how Lepke and his partner took a legitimate business and sucked the life out of it.[29] Lepke and Gurrah penetrated many legitimate businesses in the men's clothing industry either by actually buying into the business or demanding to be put on the payroll without any capital investment at all.

Flour Trucking

The foundation of this racket was the use of an employer organization known as the Flour Truckmen's Association. This group was organized by Buchalter and other racketeers for the purpose of extorting money and membership fees from flour-trucking and bakery companies in the metropolitan New York City area. The conspiracy also involved union activities such as pickets, strikes, and threats to call strikes by Local 138 of the Flour, Furniture Grocery and Bakers Supply Drivers Union, which was affiliated with the Teamsters.

Money was extorted by forcing independent truckers to join the Flour Truckmen's Association, paying membership fees and dues. Buchalter gained control of Local 138 and dominance over William Snyder, the local's president. Buchalter's man in the Flour Truckmen's Association was Danny Richter, who was business manager.[30] Strikes would be called whenever Buchalter ordered them. They would be called off only after the businessmen paid a large extortion. The rights of the workers were to be ignored. The gangsters intended to set up a trade association in every field of the industry with lawyers and front men protecting them from harm.[31]

According to later trial testimony, Lepke was reported to have said in 1931 about his interest in the baking industry, "It means to us a lot of money, maybe millions of dollars. In the flour industry, we have got the jobbers and the truckmen, and the next will be the bakers, and we are going to make it a big thing."[32]

With Lepke operatives Richter and Snyder in control of the bosses and workers in the bakery industry, the racket progressed until 1932 when legal action was initiated in the

Bronx against the Brooklyn and New York Flour Truckmen's Association by one of its members. This resulted in the collapse of the racket for about two years. This stemmed from the actions of two brothers, Aaron and Isidore Held. These were two brave flour truckers who refused to pay tribute to the racketeers. In 1930, the Helds merged their business with the M&G Trucking Company and thereafter conducted business under the name of the United Flour Trucking Corporation. Buchalter demanded $2,000 for making the merger possible. The Held brothers refused to pay. They also refused to give Buchalter through the association an additional levy of one penny for every barrel of flour carted by the corporation, which according to Held was 25,000 barrels a week.

Reacting to Buchalter's demands, Aaron Held resigned from the employers association, whereupon his drivers were called out on strike in September 1930. Held was told the strike would only end when he resumed membership in the association and agreed to pay the penny-a-barrel tribute. Aaron Held finally agreed, but in 1931, he refused to take any more orders from Buchalter and filed in the Bronx County Court a complaint charging Richter, Snyder, Buchalter, and Mathew Cantwell with extortion. Buchalter and Cantwell went on the lam while Snyder and Richter were indicted, tried on the charges, and acquitted. After the trial, Buchalter and Cantwell surrendered to authorities in the Bronx, but the indictment was dismissed.

By 1934, Buchalter, Snyder, and William "Wolfie" Goldis had resumed their racket through Local 138. The local had remained in their control and their employers association, which had been reorganized and renamed the

Flour Truckmen's Association. Max Silverman replaced Danny Richter as Buchalter's personal representative. After Richter was gone, next to go was William Snyder. Snyder, as president of Local 138, had grown independent and was not cooperating fully with Buchalter, Goldis, and Samuel Schorr. He had become an obstacle that had to be removed.[33]

On the evening of September 13, 1934, a meeting was arranged in Garfein's Restaurant at 10 Avenue A. The room was dark except for one pool of light in a front corner. Under the light, two little round tables were shoved together and around them sat fifteen men discussing the threat of a strike. Twelve of the men were connected in one way or another with the Flour Truckmen's Association, as well as being representatives of Local 138. Max Silverman; William "Wolfie" Goldis, vice president of Local 138; and other Buchalter henchmen were in attendance. They had left one vacant chair with its back toward the door for Local 138 President William Snyder. The men around the table were displeased with Snyder. He had been refusing to follow the orders of the mob.

When Snyder arrived, he was greeted by his friend, Wolfie Goldis. At about 10 P.M., a figure appeared in the restaurant and advanced out of the darkness toward the tables. He raised a pistol and shot Snyder in the back. Snyder sprang up, glanced at the gunman, and wheeled around. The assassin fired twice again. One shot went wild, but the second found its mark. Snyder lingered two days before he died. Morris Goldis, Wolfie Goldis's brother, was identified by witnesses as the gunman. The witnesses would later recant their testimony.

William "Wolfie" Goldis became president of Local

138, and he promptly put Morris on the union payroll.[34] The Goldis brothers would be tried and given light sentences for becoming state's witnesses against Lepke. According to later trial testimony, Morris Goldis claimed Lepke and Max Silverman ordered him to kill William Snyder. Goldis claimed he would have been murdered if he did not go through with the killing.[35]

In addition to the New York garment industry and the baking industry, Buchalter and Shapiro had their hands in other labor-related rackets. They were involved in the motion-picture-operators union, the leather workers, the milliners, the handbag makers, and the shoe trade. The Lepke mob provided gorillas for cabarets in a partnership with the Bug-and-Myer mob. Lepke ran the taxi racket, was a partner in the poultry workers union, and seized the restaurant racket from the Dutch Schultz mob after Schultz was murdered in 1935. Lepke was also a partner with Charles "Lucky" Luciano in the cleaning- and dyeing-industry rackets.[36]

During the time that Buchalter and Shapiro were consolidating their power in the garment industry, Buchalter became the overseer of the New York mob's new enforcement department that would become known as Murder Inc. Although this group was the mob's general enforcement arm, by the late thirties, they had in effect become Lepke Buchalter's personal group of assassins. They were used extensively as muscle in various garment-industry disputes. In the end, it would be a murder ordered by Buchalter and committed by these killers that would destroy the mob boss.

6 The Birth of Murder Inc.

*"I am not a stool pigeon. Every one of those guys wanted to talk. Only
I beat them to the bandwagon. They would be hanging me right now
if they had a chance."*[1]

—Abe "Kid Twist" Reles, 1940

With the consolidation of organized crime groups in
New York City during the early thirties, it was decided by the ruling New York mob bosses that a murder-and-mayhem department was needed. This group would
maintain discipline within the ranks of the organized-crime cartel to ensure that all moneymaking ventures
operated smoothly. Thus was born what journalists would
later refer to as "Murder Inc." Lepke became the overseer
of this group.[2]

Murder Inc., known in the New York underworld as
the "Combination," was actually comprised of two
Brooklyn gangs that formed an alliance in the early thirties to depose the Shapiro brothers. The Shapiro and
Amberg mobs controlled the rackets in what was then the
predominantly Jewish sections of Brownsville and East
New York during the twenties. Their underworld business
operations included gambling, prostitution, drug peddling, and extortion.[3]

The Brooklyn Underworld of the Twenties

In the twenties, the most-important sources of illicit income—bootlegging, drug peddling, prostitution, and gambling—were in the hands of the four Amberg brothers, Hymie, Oscar, Joey, and Louis, and the Shapiro brothers, Meyer, Irving, and Willie. Their thugs, acting as salesmen, used brass knuckles and blackjacks to persuade speakeasy owners that Amberg/Shapiro beer was the best on the market. Speakeasies had to be watched against rival beer gangs, so the Amberg/Shapiro outfit hired tough kids like Abe "Kid Twist" Reles and Harry "Happy" Maione, later leaders of the Brooklyn Combination, as guards. These underworld storm troopers also guarded beer trucks, kept a watch on stills, helped bottle bootleg gin, and pasted "tickets" (labels) on bottles. These jobs paid little, but were an important start. Where the Ambergs and Shapiros ran the show, it gave a man great prestige to work for them in any capacity.[4]

To the speakeasies came the slot machines. These in turn were owned and controlled by the Amberg/Shapiro group.

The Amberg Brothers

The Amberg brothers originally operated out of the Brownsville section of Brooklyn. Of the four Amberg brothers, three became notorious gangsters. Hyman "Hymie the Rat" Amberg was the first of the brothers to draw media attention. On July 22, 1926, Hymie shot a jeweler to death during a holdup. The jeweler, Aaron R. Rudack, had made a name for himself. The papers called him "the Fighting Jeweler" because he had effectively fought off holdup attempts on three different occasions.

Hymie was a member of a holdup gang that reportedly stole $250,000 in cash and jewelry over a period of ten months.[5]

Described by detectives as a professional thief and holdup man, Hyman Amberg was also available to do strong-arm work if the price was right. Police claimed that he had been a member of the Reece Whitmore gang of stickup men and also had done work in the garment district as a professional slugger during strikes.[6]

On November 3, 1926, Amberg and two other convicts committed suicide during an unsuccessful breakout at the Tombs Prison in Manhattan. All three prisoners shot themselves in the head after it became obvious that their escape attempt had failed.[7] A Brooklyn fish dealer later confessed that he had thrown two pistols and a quantity of ammunition over the Centre Street wall of the Tombs about ten days before the escape attempt.

Oscar Amberg was implicated as part of the jailbreak conspiracy, but was arrested and released after he denied any part in the breakout and police had insufficient evidence.[8] Louis and Joey Amberg were in prison at the time of Hymie's death.

Oscar Amberg was a labor racketeer. In 1933 in an election dominated by his brother, Louis, and assisted by Lepke and Gurrah, Oscar was made principal business agent of Local No. 102 of the Brotherhood of Painters of America. At an election held on June 7, 1933, at the Brownsville lyceum, Amberg was elected business agent.

By February 1934, the Local 102 membership was so appalled by the work of Amberg and his cronies, they sent the following letter to the American Federation of Labor (AFL).

We protest against conditions in Local No. 102 and ask you to order the General Executive Board of the Brotherhood of Painters of America to have its international officers investigate these conditions.

We ask that legal action be instituted for the removal of present officers and the ordering of a new election free from gangster methods and intimidation of workers.

Due to misdeeds and misleading on the part of the officials of Local Union No. 102 particularly Jake Wellner [Jake the Bum] and Oscar Amberg, business agents, and I. Sisselman, Chairman, our union in Brooklyn has become a nest of corruption, racketeering and gangsterism, preying on our membership, misusing our funds and collaborating with the employers to undermine union conditions and the scale of wages.

These business agents were not elected by the membership, but were forced upon them for a three year period against their will. We further demand that these business agents, Jake Wellner and Oscar Amberg, be immediately removed, together with the entire local administration and that a new election be held immediately for a one year period for all officers, this election to be supervised by a reliable organization, friendly to the labor movement.[9]

Local 102 was taken over by the Combination after Joe and Louis Amberg were disposed of in 1935.

Louis Amberg, known on the street as "Pretty" because of his ugliness, was a significant force in the New York underworld from the late twenties until 1935 when he and his brother, Joey, were murdered. Louis Amberg supposedly invented what the underworld referred to as a "bag job." His victims were stuffed into laundry bags and tied up in such a way that their struggles would strangle them.

According to one account, Louis was so ugly that it was reported that the Ringling Brothers Circus once offered him a job. They wanted him to appear as the missing link. Rather than be insulted, Amberg was flattered and often bragged about this offer.[10] Pretty Amberg and his brother, Joey, made their money in bootlegging, extortion, and loan-sharking. They also dabbled in narcotics. They were murdered in 1935 when they ran afoul of the Combination. First Joey and his bodyguard were lined up against the wall of a Brooklyn garage and shot to death. Then Louis was brutally hacked to death, and his body thrown into a stolen car and set on fire.[11]

The Shapiro brothers, mentors of the gangsters who founded Murder Inc., were also involved in bootlegging, extortion, and furnishing strong-arm men for labor disputes.

Meyer Shapiro, the oldest of the three brothers, was totally ruthless. He personally owned fifteen brothels and operated a successful loan-shark and slot-machine operation. The pinball machine racket in Brownsville was controlled by the Shapiro mob and their henchmen. The Shapiro brothers collected $5 for every pinball machine placed in Brownsville saloons and candy stores.[12]

Meyer was fearless when facing a gun, but had a deathly fear of knives. This could be the reason that his enemies on fourteen different occasions attempted to stab him to death. His enemies finally caught up with him, and on September 17, 1931, he was shot once in the head and killed. His younger brother, Irving, was murdered at the door of his apartment in July 1931.[13] The youngest brother, Willie, was murdered by the Combination in 1934.[14]

Abraham "Kid Twist" Reles (1906–1941) had worked for the Shapiro brothers in the late twenties as an enforcer. About 1930, Reles and several close friends and business associates decided to go into the slot-machine business without the approval of the Shapiro/Amberg group. They set up operations in a Brownsville candy store and began forcing local businesses to rent their slot machines.

Meyer Shapiro was furious when he learned what Reles and his friends were trying to do. His first act of retaliation was personally beating and raping Reles's fiancée. This led to open warfare between the Reles and Shapiro groups. In order to enlarge the numbers of his small gang, Reles made an alliance with a predominantly Italian Ocean Hill, Brooklyn, mob led by Harry "Happy" Maione. The two gangs would combine and go into a partnership for the operation of handbooks (horse-betting parlors) and slot machines in Brooklyn.

With this alliance of the two gangs, the Combination was born.[15] To avoid paying tax or tribute to the Shapiro brothers, the newly formed Combination relied on the power of the Bug-and-Meyer mob. A Reles mobster and friend named George DeFeo had an older brother, William, who was a powerful gangster working for the Bug-and-Meyer organization run by Benjamin "Bugsy" Siegel and Meyer Lansky. Through this organization, the Reles mob received a credit line on pinball and slot machines and began to actively place them in Brownsville locations. This, of course, resulted in the gang war and overthrow of the Shapiro brothers by the Combination.[16]

Once the Combination took over the Brooklyn rackets, its principal sources of income included the types of rackets the Shapiro brothers had controlled. Murder was only a sideline related to ensure the smooth operations of the business. The reputation of the Combination as an efficient murder machine attracted the attention of the powerful New York mob bosses.[17] As a result, the Combination became the enforcement arm of the New York mob bosses in 1931 with the blessings of Charles "Lucky" Luciano.

Murder Inc. was actually an independent enforcement group within La Cosa Nostra (the Mafia) to carry out contract killings. It was not associated directly with any particular La Cosa Nostra crime family. The idea behind the indirect association of Murder Inc. was to insulate the organized-crime bosses from any connection to specific mob-related murders. It was to have its own independent structure and personnel. Louis "Lepke" Buchalter was chosen by Luciano to be the boss of Murder Inc. He was to work through a powerful Brooklyn gangster named Albert Anastasia. Anastasia was a capo in the Mangano crime family and became the street supervisor of Murder Inc. It was Anastasia who delivered the murder contracts to Abe Reles, who in turn would assign a particular gunman for the job.[18]

The idea of retaining Murder Inc. as the official executioners for the mob is attributed to Lepke. The Combination received a retainer of $12,000 a year to ensure that staff hit men could be ready with a phone call. Because Reles and his gunmen were young, quick tempered, and volatile, it was possible that they could quarrel among themselves and even run wild if not properly controlled.

Lepke, who was a first-class administrator, as well as once a savage killer himself, was a perfect candidate to become the boss of the outfit. Reles would function as executive vice president. He would be permitted to settle local quarrels on his own initiative. But otherwise, he would only act on orders issued by Lepke.

When Lepke, acting on his own or for any other national mob, decreed an execution, Murder Inc. would carry it out. At a moment's notice, the hit man was prepared to travel anywhere in the country. The instant a murder was done, the Murder Inc. member was under orders to return to his home base in Brooklyn. That would leave the police at the scene of the murder searching for a slayer who was no longer in the vicinity. Louis Capone and Albert Anastasia were Lepke's personal representatives in Brooklyn. All contracts for murder were given to Anastasia, who in turn gave the orders to Reles.[19]

Actually, Reles had been doing work for Louis Capone and Albert Anastasia since 1928 when he was twenty-two. In that year, he frequented a café in the Ocean Hill section of Brooklyn owned by Louis Capone and his brother. Prior to 1928, Capone (no relation to Al Capone) and Anastasia had some sort of alliance or relationship, and Anastasia was a frequent visitor to the café. Reles and other young toughs such as Maione already considered Capone and Anastasia their advisers several years before the Combination was officially put under the umbrella of Lepke and the New York mob. During this time, Reles did the first of a series of favors for Anastasia and Capone. He shot somebody pointed out by Capone. Thereafter, Reles did a number of burglaries and some strong-arm work for Louis Capone.[20]

In return for murder services rendered to the New York mob, Brownsville was to be left intact. Not only would the Combination continue to control what it had, it was to take over the prostitution racket as distinguished from the shakedown of houses; the shylock racket, whereby the mob collects one dollar per week on every five dollars loaned; and the racket control of the painters union, which Reles turned over to his partner, Martin "Bugsy" Goldstein. In return for these concessions, the Reles Combination was to handle all killings ordered for all gangs, except in special cases, in which event the price was to be set in advance. There was to be no direct payment for homicides. The revenues from additional racket territory guaranteed to the Combination by the big bosses would more than cover it.[21]

Lepke gave orders to the Brooklyn gang through the years for more than thirty contracts. His personal staff more than doubled that figure in the New York area alone. (Mendy Weiss, Allie Tannenbaum, Charles Workman, and other Lepke personal staff gunmen can all be considered part and parcel of Murder Inc. killers. They were one and the same.[22])

Contracts for murder were usually given to the victim's closest friend. This would be the person the victim completely trusted. In Abe Reles's words, "Whenever they got to kill somebody they tell a guy from the Bronx or the eastside or Brooklyn, whoever knows the guy, here is the guy in this case, and here Nitzberg got the contract for 'Plug' Schuman. He knew him. If I knew the guy I would have got the contract. That is how it worked."[23]

From 1931 until Murder Inc. was finally destroyed in 1940, it was responsible for an estimated one thousand murders nationally, two hundred in the New York area alone. Abe Reles became a state witness in 1940 during the Brooklyn D.A.'s office's investigation of the local rackets. It would be the testimony of Abe Reles in 1940 that would dismantle the organization and put seven of its members in the electric chair, including boss Lepke.[24]

Up until the end of the organization, Murder Inc. operated smoothly, profitably, and with astonishing efficiency. There had never been anything like it in any civilized society. It was a government within a government; it was a suprapolice force. Once a sentence was handed down, no one escaped the consequences. There was no court of appeals, no judge to recommend mercy, no presidential pardon, no probation. It dealt with many hoodlums who had beaten the law on a dozen occasions, but no one ever beat the law of Murder Inc. The members of the mob were incredible men, unhampered by either conscience or humanity. They killed with the utmost casualness. They tortured before they killed. They mutilated corpses. They scattered bodies all across the country. Murder Inc. was in effect the enforcement branch of the Supreme Court of the underworld.[25]

With the new enforcement arm in place, Buchalter and Shapiro entered into a golden era of plunder that was not to be seriously disturbed until the late thirties.

7 The Fat Years

*"The killer who sucked at the veins of the honest working man was so
devoted that his stepson later said, 'Louis was better to me than my
own father could have been.'"*[1]

By the early thirties, Lepke and Gurrah Shapiro were
millionaires from their racket schemes. On March 20,
1931, Louis "Lepke" Buchalter married a twenty-
seven-year-old widow named Betty Wasserman. The ceremony was performed at the New York City Municipal
Building by Michael J. Cruise, the city clerk. The two witnesses were listed as P. Poveromo and Morris Wolensky.
Wolensky was a gambling partner of Buchalter's, better
known in the underworld as "Moey Dimples."[2]

Betty Wasserman Buchalter's maiden name was
Arbeiter. She was born in London, England, in 1904. Her
father, Abraham Arbeiter, was a barber, and her mother,
the former Sarah Jacobs, was born in Russia. In 1908, the
family immigrated to the U.S. Like Lepke, Betty's parents
divorced when she was a youngster. She attended grade
school and high school in New York City. In 1920, she
married World War I veteran Jacob Wasserman, who died
in 1928 as the result of an appendix operation. Prior to

her marriage to Buchalter, Betty was employed as a hostess by Ben Marden, who managed New York nightclubs.

She was also employed as the hostess at the Kentucky Club on West Forty-seventh Street in Manhattan, where she operated under the name of Betty Wilson. It was probably in one of these clubs that Betty was introduced to Lepke. An F.B.I. report stated that "Betty frequents nightclubs, keeps late hours, and plays cards and the horses to a considerable extent."[3]

Betty had one son by her first marriage, Harold, who was about eight years old when the couple was married. Lepke was known as a devoted husband and stepfather. He was extremely fond of Betty's son and carried his picture inside the back cover of the diamond-studded, platinum pocket watch he carried.

In 1934, Buchalter legally adopted Harold.[4] In the adoption papers, Lepke stated that his job was general manager of the Perfection Coat Front Manufacturing Company, 11 West Nineteenth Street, New York City, and also general manager of the Garfield Express Company, 272 Oak Street, Passaic, New Jersey. In the adoption papers, he claimed that his income was $20,000 a year.[5]

This is an interesting income figure. Crime historians and the F.B.I. estimate that by 1934, Lepke and Gurrah were splitting anywhere from $2 to $50 million a year from their various rackets. Gurrah Shapiro was a familiar figure at nightclubs, hockey games, and the racetracks. The less-flamboyant Lepke lived as a rich businessman in the luxurious Majestic Apartments overlooking Central Park West.[6] Betty Buchalter ran a novelty and handbag company to keep busy while Lepke oversaw his racket empire.[7]

The men who made up Lepke's personal entourage came from every walk of life. He only excluded those men who did his actual dirty work. Once success arrived, Lepke, who was once a shtarker himself, never admitted one into his presence. Among his personal staff was Henry "Heinzie" Tietlebaum, who was his favorite. Brought up on the Lower East Side, Heinzie had been a funeral-car driver before Lepke hired him as his personal chauffeur to handle the two Lincoln limousines he used to get about town.

Louis Kravitz was his most-trusted lieutenant. Hyman "Curly" Holtz, with whom Lepke had worked his way off the street, was also a lieutenant by seniority. Although Holtz was an experienced racketeer who knew all the angles, he was inclined to overstate his importance, often likening himself to Lepke and Gurrah as a partner rather than a hired hand. Buchalter never completely trusted Holtz, who later proved to be untrustworthy and was, therefore, eliminated.

Paul Berger was also close to Lepke and became one of his trusted subordinates. It was Berger who arranged the meetings for Lepke with various individuals in the garment industry. He also served as one of the principal collectors for Lepke's many enterprises.

Other members of Lepke's organization included Joe Amoruso, known to the clothing-industry workers he terrorized as "Joe Strawberry," a labor-union collector; Joseph Roccabono, also a labor-union collector; and Danny Fields, an ex-welterweight fighter, who was Lepke's trade-association collector and payoff man.

Since every criminal organization must expect a certain amount of police interference, advance arrangements were usually made for bail bonds. This was done for Lepke and Gurrah by the Albert brothers, operators of the Peerless Bonding Company. Herbert Albert, had two daughters. One was married to Lou Kravitz and the other to Heinzie Tietlebaum.

There was nothing static about Lepke. With the money literally pouring in, he decided to invest in a legitimate business. Along with Gurrah Shapiro, he established the firm of Leo, Greenberg and Shapiro. Lepke and Gurrah were partners and major stockholders in the Frankel Pleating Corporation. They also established the Raleigh Manufacturing Company with factories in Baltimore. This was one of the largest manufacturing plants of its kind in the world.

Life was rosy for these twin titans of crime. The entire garment industry feared them and paid heavy tribute for their favors. Their organization was functioning smoothly while their legitimate corporations were showing huge profits. According to one account, Lepke could adopt the fine manners of a gentleman, but sometimes took a certain sadistic delight in humiliating Betty in front of friends by commenting in a vulgar fashion about her personal appearance. Gurrah and his wife lived quietly with their three children in a residential section of Brooklyn.[8]

Once success arrived, Lepke and Gurrah lifted themselves off the street and into the front office. Then they began to find out how the other half lived. Lepke wintered in California or Florida and took the baths at Hot Springs, Arkansas, with one of the more-stylish groups at the Hotel Arlington, which included such underworld limelights as Charles "Lucky" Luciano, Joe Adonis, Meyer Lansky, Tammany Hall politician Jimmy Hines, and Hot

Springs host Owney Madden. The businessmen of such industries as clothing, furs, and baking, and in turn the public, footed the bill as the rackets ruler romped deluxe style.

Important underworld leaders were present at the Buchalter family celebrations. The guest list of Lepke's son Harold's bar mitzvah reads like a who's who of the underworld in 1935. Present at the party were Lucky Luciano, Abner "Longy" Zwillman, Benjamin "Bugsy" Siegel, Meyer Lansky, Tom Kutty, and Morris Wolensky.[9] Lepke and his wife traveled often to Europe where Buchalter took the baths at Carlsbad Czechoslovakia, for an ongoing kidney ailment.[10]

Lepke had a long list of acquaintances and a wide range of connections in the national underworld. He was often spoken of in underworld circles as the New York contact for the Barker Karpis gang and Verne Miller. Just how Buchalter became connected with Miller is unknown. However, it is possible that he met Miller and other Midwestern outlaws during his sojourns to Hot Springs, a favorite stop for freewheeling Midwestern bank robbers.

Another rumor had it that Verne Miller, the western gunman, was introduced to Buchalter by a New Jersey gangster named Sammy Schrager. According to this account, Buchalter and Miller met in 1929 and became fast friends. Buchalter and his wife were reported to have a warm relationship with Miller's girlfriend, Vi Mathias.

During Thanksgiving 1932, Frank Nash and Verne Miller dined with the Buchalters in their Central Park West apartment. Miller's girlfriend also did a considerable amount of traveling with Betty Buchalter in New York State and Canada. Miller may have worked for Buchalter as an assassin in the early thirties. After Miller was implicated as one of the gunmen in the Kansas City Massacre in June 1933, his visits to New York and Buchalter became a problem. It is suspected that Lepke had something to do with the murder of Verne Miller on a lonely road outside of Detroit in November 1933. It was thought that Miller's visits to New York were bringing too much heat on the mob.[11]

Even as Buchalter and Shapiro were living the good life, the seeds for the destruction of their racket empire had already been sown. Their nemesis was to come in the form of a special prosecutor named Thomas E. Dewey, who was appointed by Gov. Herbert H. Lehman in 1935 to clean up organized crime in New York City and corruption in the D.A.'s office.

8 Dewey Takes Aim

"In the 1930's and in the years that followed, it seemed to me that organized crime linked with corruption in government was the greatest single threat to our freedom in America."[1]

—Thomas E. Dewey

The nemesis of New York City organized crime in the thirties came in the person of Thomas E. Dewey. Dewey's gang-busting days as special prosecutor and district attorney of New York County represent the first truly successful effort to crush organized gangland.

Thomas E. Dewey was born in Owosso, Michigan, on March 24, 1902. He came from a long line of conservative Republican WASPs, and his father owned the local newspaper. In 1919, Dewey entered the University of Michigan, where he studied voice and became an accomplished singer.[2] In 1923, Dewey entered Columbia Law School and upon completing his studies, went to work for a Wall Street law firm.

As a Midwestern Republican WASP in Jimmy Walker's New York of the twenties, Dewey was drawn into reform politics.[3] Early in his career, the law firm that employed him retained a distinguished New York City attorney, George Z. Medalie, to represent one of its clients. Dewey worked with Medalie preparing the case, and Medalie was greatly impressed with the young man's legal ability. On February 12, 1931, Medalie was sworn in as U.S. Attorney for the Southern District of New York and appointed Dewey to the post of chief assistant. As Assistant U.S. Attorney, Dewey gained invaluable experience in the preparation and trial of important criminal cases, as well as in the administration of an important prosecutor's office. He also developed background information on New York City organized crime and the close association that existed between racketeers and Tammany Hall political leaders.

By 1933, the U.S. Attorney's Office was ready to proceed with income-tax prosecutions of two of the city's more-affluent gang leaders, Arthur Flegenheimer (Dutch Schultz) and Irving Wexler (Waxey Gordon). Schultz was charged with evading $92,103 in federal taxes on an estimated income of $481,000. Schultz went on the lam and could not be located for prosecution.

On November 1, 1933, George Z. Medalie resigned as U.S. Attorney and returned to private practice. Through the authority of a seldom-used federal statute, a U.S. district judge designated Dewey, then thirty-one-years old, to serve as acting U.S. Attorney until such time as a successor was appointed by the president.[4] With Dewey personally handling the prosecution, the income-tax evasion trial of Waxey Gordon began on November 20, 1933. At the conclusion of the nine-day trial, Gordon was convicted on all counts and sentenced to ten years in federal prison.[5]

On November 25, 1933, President Franklin Roosevelt announced the appointment of Martin T. Conboy as the new U.S. Attorney for the Southern District of New York, and Dewey returned to private practice.

By the mid-1930s, it was conservatively estimated that organized underworld rackets cost the city of New York a billion dollars a year. The federal government was able to go after Prohibition-era racketeers, although in most cases futilely, because there were laws in place that allowed the feds to get involved. Although organized crime had national ramifications as early as the midtwenties, most rackets were local affairs. Often gangsters kept their machinations well within the limits of a single state or city. There were no RICO laws (Racketeer Influenced Corrupt Organizations law, 1970). A number of cities and states enacted public-enemy laws, which had penalties that were little more than a slap on the wrist. In most cases, these local predecessors of RICO were struck down by state courts as unconstitutional. The federal government's jurisdiction could seldom be invoked in the thirties.

As for city governments, they did nothing against organized crime for a variety of reasons, but chiefly because the racketeer always paid his way. In New York City, he was a member of a Tammany Hall club. Tammany Hall was the city's Democratic political machine. Gangsters were useful on Election Day when plug uglies could be counted on for strong-arm work at the polls and between elections. They made substantial contributions to various Tammany Hall politicians' war chests. As a result, well-connected underworld figures were good friends of the local political leaders, the right police, the magistrates, and even better, may have a powerful district leader as a partner.

For many years, the D.A.'s office of New York County was regarded as the special plum of one or two powerful Tammany Hall district leaders whose special province was commercialized vice, gambling, prostitution, and liquor. One way of using the office was to name a pliant tool. Another way was to name a respectable nonentity to the office.

Judge C. T. Crain was a good example. He had been a Supreme Court justice. He was eminently respectable, but he had already reached retirement age as judge. At a time when he was a candidate for his slippers, pipe, and memoirs, he was named to the turbulent job of prosecutor of New York County, which called for the energy and resourcefulness of a youthful, robust, and energetic man.

In the fall of 1933, a grand jury began to pry into some of the industrial rackets in New York City. The grand jury got nowhere with the D.A.'s office, which did not seem to be cooperating in the investigation. In March 1934, another grand jury began a similar examination. By this time, a new D.A. was in office, William Copeland Dodge. Dodge had been a Tammany magistrate and was a member of one of the Tammany Hall clubs frequented by racketeers. This grand jury soon became convinced that Mr. Dodge's assistants were not giving much help in the fight against organized crime.[6] The Manhattan D.A. would not cooperate, so the jury bolted. It excluded the D.A.'s men from proceedings and became what is often referred to as a runaway grand jury. They defied the Tammany Hall D.A., claiming the machine was protecting Dutch Schultz and other mobsters, and demanded that Gov. Herbert Lehman, a Democrat, appoint a special prosecutor.[7]

On June 25, 1935, the governor forwarded to D.A. Dodge the names of four outstanding Republican attorneys, George Z. Medalie, Charles E. Hughes Jr., Charles H. Tuttle, and Thomas D. Thatcher, and directed him to designate one of them as special prosecutor. All declined, but in a special statement to Governor Lehman on June 26, 1935, they unanimously urged that the governor appoint Thomas E. Dewey to the post. Initially, Governor Lehman rejected their recommendation on the grounds that Dewey was not widely enough known, but then yielded to pressure, and Dewey was appointed special prosecutor.

The special prosecutor promptly recruited an unusually able staff of twenty deputy assistant prosecutors, ten investigators, and ten accountants, as well as process servers, stenographers, and clerical personnel.[8] Unlike Dodge, Dewey had no allegiance to Tammany Hall politicians who often protected racketeers. He set up offices in the Woolworth Building.[9]

Office space was offered to Dewey in various public buildings. But they were potential open sieves for secrets. Other prosecutors had been unable to move without publicity. So Dewey took space, 10,500 square feet of it, on the fourteenth floor of the Woolworth Building near City Hall. Here, there were many entrances and exits, passenger and freight elevators—too many for underworld spies to cover completely—and such throngs of people rushing in and out that it was all but impossible to spot individuals. A twenty-four-hour guard of police was posted in the building. In the offices, there was every device for the concealment of witnesses. There were venetian blinds on the windows and frosted glass in the partitions of the numerous waiting rooms. A telephone cable that could not be tapped was connected directly with the main office of the telephone company. All stenographic work was done in one large room under inspection. Special locks replaced the standard variety on the filing cabinets. Every device security experience had found desirable was installed.[10]

Dewey began his work as special prosecutor with general targets: the industrial rackets, policy gambling, and prostitution. Dutch Schultz controlled policy (numbers betting) in Harlem and the Bronx. As an assistant U.S. Attorney, Dewey had attempted to prosecute Schultz for income-tax evasion. Schultz fled the indictment and later gave himself up after Dewey had left the federal prosecutor's office. He was acquitted on the tax-evasion charge.

By 1935, Schultz was the last major non-Italian mobster still functioning on his own.[11] Schultz was also heavily involved in labor racketeering in the restaurant industry of New York City. Early in 1932, Schultz mobsters took control of two waiters unions to which all restaurant employees in the city were forced to pay dues. Schultz mobsters then created an employers association known as the Metropolitan Restaurant and Cafeteria Association. All restaurant and cafeteria owners were forced to join this organization or face the consequences. Failure to join resulted in strikes, picket lines, stench bombs, and beatings.[12]

Dewey started to put together an airtight case against Schultz in the restaurant shakedown racket. The special prosecutor also investigated the Schultz mob's control over the numbers racket in New York City. Seven men would eventually go to prison in the restaurant racket. These were a combination of Schultz minions and crooked labor leaders.[13]

Not surprisingly, as a result of his investigation, Dewey incurred the animosity of Dutch Schultz. Dewey was pursuing the mobster with a vengeance. After Schultz had been acquitted of tax evasion, he planned to return to New York City. Mayor Fiorello LaGuardia, however, warned Schultz to stay out of the city. As a result, the gangster set up headquarters in the Palace Chop House, a Newark, New Jersey, restaurant. From his base of operations, he directed his mob's New York City rackets.

Schultz was infuriated over the new legal assault and decided to murder the special prosecutor. He called a meeting of the New York mob bosses to discuss the feasibility of such a plan. A hypothetical murder plot was hatched at the meeting. It was also decided that before Dewey was murdered, someone would follow him on his daily rounds to see if there was a time that the special prosecutor would be most vulnerable to an assassin. Reportedly, Albert Anastasia, posing as a proud father walking his infant in a baby buggy, posted himself in Dewey's neighborhood and watched the special prosecutor go through his daily routine for a week. (It is more likely that an unknown person working for Anastasia cased Dewey.) Anastasia by 1935 was a widely known gangster in the city and could have been recognized. The story may very well have been embellished later by Anastasia.[14]

Every morning, Dewey left his apartment with two bodyguards and went to a nearby drugstore to make his daily business calls from a pay phone. He believed his home phone was tapped by underworld technicians. Dewey was always accompanied by his two detective bodyguards. The two police officers would remain outside the drugstore while the prosecutor went in and used the phone. Anastasia believed that a gunman equipped with a pistol and silencer could be waiting in the drugstore before Dewey arrived. The assassin would wait until Dewey entered the phone booth and shoot the prosecutor. He would then kill the pharmacist, put his gun back in his coat, and casually walk past the two detectives stationed outside.

Anastasia reported on Dewey's movements at a second meeting of New York mob bosses. After giving the plan further thought, Luciano and Lepke decided against it. They reasoned that the murder of Dewey would result in a public outcry and in turn a law-enforcement crackdown on the rackets that would hurt everyone. Buchalter was reported to have said, "This is the worst thing in the world. It will hit us all in the pocketbooks because everybody will come down on our heads." Elsewhere, Lepke is quoted as saying, "We will all burn if Dewey is knocked off."

Schultz stormed out of the meeting, vowing to personally kill Dewey. A vote was taken, and it was decided to take steps to save the prosecutor by killing Schultz. On the night of October 23, 1935, Schultz and three associates were shot to death at the Palace Chop House in Newark by Emanuel "Mendy" Weiss and Charles "Bug" Workman, two of Lepke's most-efficient personal staff killers. The getaway car driver was an underworld character known only as "Piggy," who was supposed to point out Schultz to the hit men.[15] With the death of Dutch Schultz, Luciano took over the policy rackets, and Lepke stepped into Schultz's restaurant shakedowns.

Early in 1936, Dewey began laying plans to strike at one of New York City's most-powerful underworld bosses, Charles "Lucky" Luciano, who had been reaping huge profits from drugs, the Italian lottery, and policy. Word on the street was that he also controlled prostitution in the city. In January 1936, Dewey investigators learned that a single combination run by Luciano had taken over the prostitution racket. Facts related to that racket were presented to the grand jury, which returned a ninety-count indictment against Luciano and fifteen conspirators.[16] On June 7, 1936, the jury returned verdicts of guilty against Luciano and his codefendants. Luciano was found guilty on sixty-two counts of the indictment and sentenced to thirty to fifty years in prison.[17]

The Dewey probe into organized crime in New York City lit fires under the federal law-enforcement community. Lepke and Gurrah were arrested and finally tried on the Sherman antitrust charges that had been pending since 1933. They were originally indicted for racketeering in the fur industry and charged with violation of the Sherman Antitrust Act for gaining control of the vast rabbit-skin industry in New York City, whose products were fur coats and pieces of fur known as "lapin." Their Protective Fur Dressing Corporation had forced every dealer, trucker hauling furs, manufacturer of pelts, and every individual in the entire business in New York City to pay tribute to them over a period of years.[18]

In an opening address to the jury on October 26, 1936, Assistant Federal Prosecutor John Harlan Aman stated that Lepke and Gurrah Shapiro had been responsible for beatings and violence in 1932 and 1933. This was a time when the Protective Fur Dressers Corporation through its membership handled between twenty and thirty million rabbit skins a year, valued at about $14 million.[19] Defense counsel argued that the communist Fur Workers Union had actually committed the acts of violence attributed to the Lepke and Gurrah mob. They contended that the effort to involve the two gangsters was a frame-up.[20]

Buchalter and Shapiro were found guilty at 12:35 A.M. Sunday, November 8, 1936, after the jury deliberated for thirty-two-and-a-half hours.[21] On November 12, 1936, the two men were sentenced by federal Judge John Knox to serve two years in federal prison and pay fines of $10,000 each. Buchalter and Shapiro were convicted on all four counts of the indictment. This represented the first conviction in the industrial-rackets case.[22] Judge Knox refused bail to the two Gorilla Boys, reasoning that racket czars of this magnitude would forgo bail forfeitures as a means of escaping justice. To them, it would be just an incidental expense.[23]

The two racketeers filed an appeal. Thomas E. Dewey was getting close to an indictment of his own against sixteen racketeers whose take from the garment industry exceeded $17 million a year. Lepke and Gurrah were at the top of the list. Dewey hurried to see federal Court of Appeals Judge Martin T. Manton when he heard that defense attorneys were asking for bail for Lepke and Gurrah while the conviction was appealed. Dewey laid out his evidence in the garment-center racketeering case he was preparing, explaining that anything less than $50,000 bail each would never hold the Gorilla Boys once they realized what was in store for them. Manton listened sympathetically, nodded in agreement, and within twenty-four hours let the men out on $10,000 bail each.[24]

Trial errors alleged by defense attorneys were in the explanation given by Judge Manton for releasing Lepke and Gurrah on bail. "Admission to bail after conviction is a matter of judicial discretion. Judge Manton's judicial discretion has been on several occasions severely criticized. It seems to us that the anti-racket drive calls for judicial wisdom and discretion of a kind very different from Judge Manton's when convicted racketeers of the big money class seek freedom on bail," screamed the *New York World-Telegram*.[25]

Even at this time, it was reported that the underworld associates of Buchalter and Shapiro advised them to contest their conviction, but to serve their sentences if necessary to keep out of the hands of Thomas E. Dewey, who in early 1936 began his investigation into New York City's industrial rackets.[26]

In the meantime, Special Prosecutor Dewey was able to link an old loan of $25,000 to Judge Manton as being from Lepke and Gurrah, the price of their release on ridiculously low bail and an example of a lengthy list of cases in which Manton sold his judgments, reaping more than $400,000 in the process.[27] On January 20, 1939, Manton was forced to resign from the federal bench because of well-founded charges of corruption that had been placed against him. He was later prosecuted and sentenced to two years in prison.[28]

Assembling his case against Lepke and Gurrah, Dewey decided to focus on their takeover of the flour-trucking and baking industry of New York City in the early thirties.[29] In the midst of Dewey's investigation of the industrial rackets, the prosecutor received letters from the mother and wife of William Snyder, president of Local 138 of the

Flour Truckmen's Union, who had been murdered September 13, 1934, when he was set up at Gurfein's Restaurant on the Lower East Side. Two witnesses identified Morris Goldis, a brother of William "Wolfie" Goldis, vice president of Local 138, as the gunman. The getaway car was traced through license plates to a man who admitted renting the car with money given him by Morris Goldis. The attorney hired to represent Morris Goldis and the man who rented the getaway car was Charles A. Schneider, then an assistant attorney general of the state of New York. Suddenly, the key witnesses recanted their identification of Morris, and the case collapsed.

Dewey's staff initiated a thorough investigation of the Flour Truckmen's Association and its covert relationship with the union. Indictments charging conspiracy were returned against Max Silverman, a son of Harold Silverman, who was a racketeer and a senior associate of Lepke and Gurrah; William "Wolfie" Goldis; and Benjamin Spivack, attorney for the Flour Truckmen's Association. All were found guilty of racketeering.

Lepke and Gurrah were fugitives and could not be found at this time. The Goldis brothers had another worry. They entertained well-grounded fears that the charge of murder was about to be leveled at them in the William Snyder case. This fear mounted when Max Rubin, a longtime right-hand man of Lepke and an associate of Max Silverman, began talking to Dewey. Rubin, a silver-haired, well-educated labor organizer, appeared before the grand jury on September 27, 1937, and fully discussed activities carried on in behalf of Lepke in the bakery racket. In the course of his testimony, he cited facts that revealed close ties between the underworld and

Tammany Hall political leaders in New York City. Rubin described how in 1935 he had collected $10,000 to settle a strike called by Local 138 against the Gottfried Baking Company. The shakedown money was paid to the office of William Solomon, then a Tammany district leader in Harlem and a satellite of Tammany politician Jimmy Hines. On orders from Lepke, Rubin paid Solomon $1,000, and Solomon, in turn, gave $500 to Sam Kantor, a lieutenant of Solomon's in the district.[30]

By midsummer of 1937, authorities were closing in on Gurrah and Lepke. The Gorilla Boys decided that it would be expedient to become fugitives. At the time of his flight, Lepke was on the payroll of the Amalgamated Clothing Workers Union, had an interest in twenty-three dress firms, and was a partner in three large trucking concerns.[31]

Shapiro became a fugitive when his federal sentence was affirmed by the U.S. Court of Appeals on June 14, 1937. Buchalter's conviction in the first federal antitrust case was reversed by the federal Court of Appeals. The government then proceeded to try Buchalter for violation of the federal antitrust laws again for his activities in the Fur Dressers Factor Corporation, another racketeering front for the Gorilla Boys. Lepke failed to appear in federal court for the Southern District of New York on July 6, 1937, forfeiting $3,000 bail and becoming a fugitive.[32]

Lepke's problems multiplied while he was in hiding. A grand jury directed by the Manhattan D.A. indicted Lepke and Gurrah Shapiro for bakery extortion. The Justice Department announced that it was rewriting the antitrust indictments with the intention of bringing Lepke to trial on new racketeering charges. The Federal Bureau of

Narcotics now entered the picture, as well. Evidence had been uncovered that Lepke was the man behind a massive drug-smuggling ring that involved the bribery of U.S. Customs officials and had smuggled at least $10 million worth of heroin into the United States from the Far East.[33]

One day in June 1937, federal narcotics Commissioner Harry Anslinger received a letter from an anonymous source suggesting that if the commissioner wanted some information on Lepke's involvement in the dope racket, the writer would be glad to cooperate. Two days later, the woman who had written the letter called Anslinger and set up a meeting. The information that was given was so well prepared that by December 1937, thirty-one people, including Lepke, were indicted for conspiracy to smuggle drugs into the Port of New York in the baggage of gang members posing as tourists. The conspiracy had been born in 1935 shortly after an explosion destroyed a heroin plant in the Bronx operated by international smuggler and bootlegger Jacob "Yasha" Katzenberg, Jake Lvovsky, and Sam Gross.[34]

This phase of the life and works of Lepke began on the afternoon of February 25, 1935, at 2919 Seymour Avenue in the Bronx, when an explosion in the apartment of a chemist named Pietro Quinto destroyed a heroin-synthesizing plant. Searching the wreckage, narcotics agents found 1,100 ounces of morphine valued at $117,000 in street prices.

Quinto, who was a member of the Katzenberg dope ring, had been hired to process the raw heroin at a salary of $50 a week. Quinto was obviously supplementing his income with some of the narcotics, as authorities found $37,000 in cash in his safe-deposit box. On November

30, 1937, an indictment of thirty people was handed up charging them with participation in a heroin-smuggling ring. Lepke was named as a principal. Another principal in the indictment was Jacob "Yasha" Katzenberg, who was already so notorious that he had been branded an international menace by the League of Nations. Katzenberg would later plead guilty to the charges and receive a sentence of ten years after being extradited on a fugitive warrant from Greece. His sentence was reduced as a result of his testimony against Lepke.[35]

Seeking new sources of supply and some ideas on running drugs, Katzenberg and Lvovsky sought Lepke's ear at a dinner party in the apartment of mutual friend and Lepke lieutenant, Lou Kravitz, in 1935. Lepke was interested. He suggested the boys get in touch with one Joe Schwartz in Mexico City and "tell him you're a friend of mine." Lepke also stated that he had some ideas about how to get the stuff into the country, which he would divulge later after Katzenberg and Lvovsky had set up a smuggling organization through Schwartz. Katzenberg went to Mexico City, connected with Schwartz, and the two men then took off for Shanghai, where Schwartz contacted a couple of Greek expatriates representing heroin dealers. Meanwhile, Lvovsky and Gross interviewed and hired a crew of carriers who would transport the junk from Shanghai to the Port of New York.

Now Lepke divulged his master plan. It was to bribe U.S. Customs inspectors at the Port of New York to sell the gang a supply of customs stamps to affix to the baggage containing the heroin. Lepke assigned a couple of his men to handle this matter and assured Lvovsky and Gross that they could start sending the tourists back with the heroin as soon as they could book passage.

As the brains of the drug-smuggling conspiracy, Lepke made no investment. He simply muscled in. His share was 50 percent of all profits from the original importation plus 50 percent of all profits following their secondary distribution to addicts. Lepke ruled that this secondary distribution would be made by an old pal who he ordered to buy up every grain of heroin the gang brought into the country.

The scheme worked beautifully from October 1935 to February 1937. Seven smuggling voyages were made by the gang's couriers on such respectable ships as the *Queen Mary*, *Berengaria*, *Majestic*, and *Aquitania*. More than $200,000 worth of pure heroin worth $10 million at the retail level was smuggled into the Port of New York in trunks bearing the appropriate customs stamps. The procedure never varied because there was no need to tamper with success.

In China, the heroin was hidden away in two wardrobe trunks that accompanied the courier as passenger baggage to France via the Suez Canal. In order to escape the prying eyes of French customs officers, the trunks were transferred from Marseilles to Cherbourg and then put on a ship sailing for the U.S.

Once the ship arrived at the Port of New York, the final stage of the smugglers' journey was accomplished through the cooperation of two U.S. customs officers. The inspectors sold clearance stamps to the gang for $1,000 a trip. (Lepke had actually feared that they might hold out for $1,500 a trip.) The customs stamps were printed in eight different colors. Different colors were used for different days in the week. One thing Lepke couldn't buy was advance notice on the color scheme to be used on any given day.

The trunks carrying the junk were not declared in the passenger's baggage declaration, but were placed on the dock under his initial. Lvovsky, carrying the customs stamps in his pocket, would mingle with the pier visitors and locate the trunks containing the heroin. Then he would casually sit down, first on one trunk, then on another. When Lvovsky left the pier, the trunks bore the proper customs stamps for the day in question. Once safely through customs, the trunks were taken to the house of one of the gang members. The heroin was picked up later by a representative of Lepke's mob. Buchalter would get his cut the same day. Nor did Lepke suffer when the last load of heroin, worth an estimated $120,000 wholesale, was mysteriously hijacked from the pier. He insisted on being paid off by Katzenberg, not only on what he would have received from the wholesale disposal to his pal, but also on the retail distribution.

Some of the more suspicious members of the smuggling gang thought that it was one of Lepke's men who hijacked the shipment (likely Hyman "Curly" Holtz, who disappeared around the same time).

The sixth of seven total shipments came up missing. It has never been definitely ascertained just what happened to it. The belief in underworld circles was that Hyman "Curly" Holtz, Lepke's longtime lieutenant, connived with the crooked customs inspectors and hijacked the load. At any rate, shortly after this incident, Curly disappeared as if whisked from the face of the earth.[36]

By the fall of 1937, narcotics agents had their hands on a kilogram of heroin with Shanghai markings, which they could prove had been part of a shipment that arrived on the *Aquitania* in May 1937.[37] Attractive, young women with winning personalities were employed by the gang as couriers to do the actual smuggling. They were paid $2,000 plus expenses to make the voyage to Europe to pick up the trunks after they had been shipped to France from China and bring them to New York.[38] Sometimes the tourists would pose as husband and wife. The U.S. Customs officers arrested in the indictment handed down November 30, 1937 were identified as Charles Barrett, Al Hoffman, and John McAdams.[39] In November 1938, John McAdams, former U.S. Customs sergeant of patrol, was convicted of bribery and sentenced by federal Judge Henry W. Goddard to serve seven years in federal prison. Hoffman got eighteen months.[40]

On April 14, 1938, Jacob "Gurrah" Shapiro surrendered to federal authorities in New York City. He claimed he was tired of being chased. At this time, he had rewards on his head totaling $7,500.[41] When Shapiro turned himself in, D.A. Thomas Dewey was preparing to bring him before Supreme Court Justice Ferdinand Pecora for arraignment in two existing indictments. It was rumored that Dewey might also ask for an indictment linking Shapiro with the 1934 murder of Teamsters Local 138 President William Snyder.

Shapiro was also ordered by federal Judge John Knox to begin serving his two-year term for his Sherman antitrust law conviction in 1937.[42] Arraigned before Judge Knox on yet-another antitrust charge charging racketeering in the New York City fancy-fur industry, Shapiro pleaded not guilty, and his trial was scheduled to begin May 11, 1938.[43]

More information came out exposing Gurrah and Lepke's attempt to put up $25,000 to fix the case against Morris Goldis in Snyder's murder. The Goldis brothers, together with Max Silverman and Sam Schorr, were now indicted by Dewey on first-degree murder charges in the death of Snyder. All agreed to turn state's evidence against their masters, Lepke and Gurrah, in return for leniency.

According to the now-singing gangsters, Snyder was killed because he refused to yield to Lepke and Gurrah's demands to join them in racketeering in the flour-trucking business.[44] This was not entirely true. Snyder had worked with the Gorilla Boys in the beginning, but had a disagreement with Lepke over calling a strike. As early as 1931, William Snyder and Lepke mobsters Danny Richter and Mathew Cantwell were indicted for extortion and acquitted.

Lepke and Gurrah were also indicted, but disappeared and did not return until their three colleagues were acquitted. Lepke and Gurrah then turned themselves in. For a couple of years, the Gorilla Boys focused on the garment industry, and Snyder got used to thinking for himself. This independent thinking proved to be the beginning of the end for him.[45] The Goldis brothers would later explain to D.A. Dewey that they were forced to kill Snyder. If they had refused, they would have been killed. On the surface, this sounded reasonable, yet both Goldis brothers benefited by Snyder being put out of the way. Remember, William "Wolfie" Goldis, vice president of Local 138, became president after Snyder's death and immediately put his brother, Morris, on the union payroll.

On June 17, 1938, Jacob "Gurrah" Shapiro was found guilty by a jury in U.S. district court on a new Sherman-antitrust-violation charge and sentenced to three more years in federal prison and a $15,000 fine. The indictment on which Shapiro was tried charged that he and several other defendants, including Lepke, who could not be found for trial, conspired to restrain trade in the $78-million fancy-fur dressing industry by intimidation and violence. The maximum sentence that could have been given was four years and a $20,000 fine. Shapiro was, however, serving two years for his 1937 conviction for racketeering in the rabbit-skin dressing industry.[46]

Dewey, who had a pending indictment against Shapiro and Buchalter charging racketeering in the flour-trucking and garment industry, indicated that he intended on trying Gurrah regardless of the federal conviction.

Shapiro made the following public statement at the close of the trial that brought his second conviction for violating the federal antitrust laws. "They arrest me because they want to be the D.A. or even governor. They don't go after the little fellows, they go after the big shots like me because the publicity I get is worth maybe $50 million. I got a good business, and I pay income tax on $30,000 a year. I don't have to commit no crimes!"[47]

As all this drama was unfolding, Lepke remained on the lam. Protected by Albert Anastasia, Lepke evaded federal and local law-enforcement authorities in what became a national and international manhunt for more than two years. More than one million wanted posters were distributed nationally. D.A. Thomas Dewey publicly called Lepke the worst industrial racketeer in America and proclaimed that the city of New York would pay a $25,000 reward to anyone who could bring in Buchalter, dead or alive.

J. Edgar Hoover, apparently alarmed that so many others, including Harry Anslinger, chief of the Bureau of Narcotics, and Lewis Valentine, New York City police commissioner, were stealing headlines, also posted a reward. Hoover stated that the feds would pay $5,000 for anyone who could bring in Buchalter, whom he described as "the most dangerous criminal in the U.S."[48]

Lepke always believed that indictments went away when witnesses disappeared. Now from his hideout in Brooklyn, he would conduct a reign of terror on potential Dewey witnesses against him. Over the more than two-year period that Lepke was a fugitive, an estimated sixty to one hundred underworld characters in the New York area disappeared completely. Some became brutally murdered corpses left in conspicuous places as a warning to potential Dewey witnesses. Others ended up in shallow graves covered with quick lime to help the body decompose. Anastasia, sometimes referred to as the "Lord High Executioner," gave the contracts to Murder Inc. killers who stalked their prey, sometimes killing the wrong person. It was Lepke's paranoia and the chaos that this caused in the underworld that in the end would destroy him.

9 No Witnesses, No Indictments

"In my judgement the community is faced with an organized effort to eliminate all former gangster associates of Lepke and Gurrah."[1]
—Thomas E. Dewey

"Those bastards are more interested in their own take than they are in my hide."[2]
—Louis "Lepke" Buchalter

From July 1937 until August 1939, federal and local law-enforcement authorities conducted an international manhunt for Buchalter.[3] Buchalter spent most of his time moving from one hideout to another in Brooklyn. Forced to be a fugitive, Lepke tried to make the best of the situation. There is some evidence that Lepke and Gurrah Shapiro spent a short time together in a hideout in New Jersey. Afterward, Lepke was moved to a room in the Oriental Danceland building at 2780 Stillwell Avenue in Brooklyn's Coney Island section. The owner of the Oriental Danceland was Zaccarino Cavitola, a relative of Louis Capone's by marriage. Zaccarino was often referred to as "Big Zack."[4]

Throughout his time on the lam, Lepke was protected and his interests were looked after by Albert Anastasia, a capo in the Mangano crime family and the overseer of the Brooklyn underworld assassin group, Murder Inc. Abe Reles of the Brooklyn Combination became the contact man for anyone who wanted to see Buchalter during his time as a fugitive. Reles would become a state witness in the Murder Inc. prosecutions in 1940. It was then that Reles disclosed details of how Lepke continued operating his racket empire while in hiding.

According to Reles, he first learned of Lepke being a fugitive when he read the papers. Sometime in 1937, the exact date he could not recall, he was standing on "the corner." The corner was located at the intersection of Saratoga and Livonia avenues in Brooklyn. This was head-quarters of Murder Inc. and a favorite hangout for Brooklyn hoodlums.

Reles claimed he was picked up by Harry "Pittsburgh Phil" Strauss, a top Murder Inc. killer, and Louis Capone. To the best of Reles's recollection, this was in the spring of 1937, as he recalled he had on a topcoat and had returned from Florida in April. He believed that his first contact with Lepke was sometime afterward. They drove to a house where Lepke was conducting a meeting.

According to Reles, Lepke did most of the talking. The meeting was about some trouble in the Brooklyn painters union. Martin Buggsy Goldstein, Reles's partner, was in jail. The discussion focused on how they would make bond for Goldstein. Lepke was also under a lot of stress as he stated that Dewey was getting very hot in his investigations of extortion in the baking and flour-trucking industries.

Reles claimed that he attended another meeting in New Jersey. At this meeting, Gurrah Shapiro was also present. Shapiro stated that he was not worried about what the feds had against him, but that he was very worried about what Dewey might have on him. At this meeting, there was discussion, particularly by Mendy Weiss, Lepke's second in command, about taking care of possible Dewey witnesses against Shapiro, meaning that they intended killing whomever they thought were the most-prominent witnesses against Gurrah in the Dewey investigation.

Reles and Harry Strauss were probably brought to this meeting to be given contracts to assassinate some of the witnesses. Reles later stated that he believed that while Gurrah Shapiro was on the lam, he stayed at the Lyndhurst, New Jersey, home of gangster Jimmy Feracco.

The next meeting that Reles had with Lepke was either in December 1938 or January 1939. His memory was not clear on the date. At this time, Louis Capone picked up Reles and drove him to the Oriental Danceland in Coney Island. On the way over in Capone's Cadillac, he explained that they were going to visit Lepke and that Lepke had been living at the Oriental Danceland. According to Reles, Lepke was living in an upstairs room in the building to which Capone had a key. Lepke complained to Capone and Reles at this time that he was "red hot," describing the manhunt against him and that all of his friends appeared to be welshing on him and wanted no part of him. After spending some time discussing other problems with Lepke, the three men ate dinner.

After this initial meeting at the Oriental Danceland, Reles stated that he saw Lepke at the Oriental Danceland every week and made at least fifteen or twenty visits to the fugitive at that location. Every time Reles went to see Lepke, he would bring a box of Corona cigars and a box of candy (Sherry's).

According to Reles, Louis Capone, Harry Strauss, and Emanuel "Mendy" Weiss had access to Lepke's apartment whenever they wanted to use it. It was Reles who first explained to F.B.I. agents that he believed that Albert Anastasia was the guiding figure behind all arrangements for the harboring of Lepke and was the broker for any murder contracts given by Lepke to eliminate potential witnesses.[5]

While Lepke was in hiding, law-enforcement efforts to find him grew at a fevered pitch. For the first time in the history of the New York City Police Department, a special squad of twenty detectives was set up to do nothing but hunt for the fugitive.[6] This squad was increased to fifty detectives by New York City Police Commissioner Louis Valentine.[7] The New York City municipal government posted a reward for $25,000 on Lepke. The U.S. government posted a reward of $5,000.[8] The feds quickly increased their reward offer to match the city of New York, bringing the total price on Lepke's head to $50,000.[9] The rewards and the constant pressure from local and federal law-enforcement agencies on the underworld created the so-called "Big Heat." This was designed so that the underworld would put pressure on Lepke to surrender.[10]

Usually, anyone desiring an audience with Lepke while he was in hiding would contact Abe Reles on the "corner," the intersection of Saratoga and Livonia avenues in Brooklyn, the headquarters of Murder Inc.[11] If the person had the right underworld credentials and was cleared by Weiss, Anastasia, and Capone, he would be driven to Buchalter's hideout.

Reles told F.B.I. agents during his 1940 debriefing that the reason that the Brownsville mob (Murder Inc.) provided such great assistance to Lepke was in return for favors Lepke had done for them in the past, such as taking care of witnesses and splitting fifty-fifty with the Brownsville mob for any extortion schemes in the garment industry in which Lepke's organization and Murder Inc. were involved. Reles claimed that to the best of his knowledge, there was a kickback of a few cents on any dresses or garments manufactured in New York City. This kickback was split three ways between the Lepke mob, Brownsville mob, and Anastasia.

After February 10, 1939, Lepke moved from the Oriental Danceland apartment to a new hideout at 2720 Foster Avenue in Brooklyn. Lepke was moved because there had been several murders within the plasterers union in Brooklyn.[12] Louis Capone was connected to the plasterers union through his brother, Sam, who was a union delegate. Two plasterers, Cesare Lattaro and Antonio Siciliano, had been ordered to kill a union dissident named Calogero Viruso, who had the nerve to openly protest kickbacks paid to union racketeers. The Capones resented this, believing that the complaining could cause dissention among the other workers.

Lattaro and Siciliano refused to go through with the murder. At the request of Louis Capone, Anastasia put out contracts on them. On the night of February 6, 1939, Harry "Happy" Maione, Frank Abbundando, and Julie Catalano pulled up to the plasterers' apartment in Brooklyn. Maione was the leader of the Italian gang from Ocean Hill that was part of the Combination. Abbundando was his lieutenant and Catalano a Maione gofer. Cruising the street that night as a backup gunman was Vito Gurino, a deadly Combination assassin.

Lattaro and Siciliano had reputations as womanizers. In a perfectly executed hit typical of the attention to detail

Murder Inc. killers paid to their work, the slightly built Maione, dressed in woman's clothes, knocked on the door of the plasterers' apartment. Maione was described as wearing a white blouse, black skirt, and a black hat with a feather in it.[13] When the men saw what they thought was a young woman standing outside their door, they opened it, at which time Maione and Abbundando burst in and blasted away with .38 revolvers, killing both men, then escaping in a stolen car driven by Catalano with Gurino following in a crash car (a vehicle whose only purpose was to block pursuing police).[14]

As a result of these murders, Louis Capone feared that the police would come to the Oriental Danceland looking for him and accidentally stumble onto Lepke's hideout. Until Lepke was moved to the Foster Avenue address, Louis Capone made himself prominent around the dance hall and would stand or sit in front of the building so that the police would readily see him and pick him up without searching the rest of the building.[15]

The Foster Avenue apartment had been rented by a Mrs. Dorothy Walker. Mrs. Walker's husband was a small-time gangster named Simon "Fatty" Walker, whose only claim to fame was being shot down by "Legs" Diamond and Charles Entratta in 1928. Diamond and Entratta were silent partners in the Hotsy Totsy Club, a fashionable speakeasy. Walker and two friends had entered the club already drunk and caused a commotion. When the owners tried to throw them out, a shouting match ensued. Walker and a friend were shot down at the bar. Another friend of Walker's was shot and kicked down the stairwell of the club, but lived.[16]

On December 2, 1940, more than a year after Lepke

gave himself up, agents questioned Mrs. Walker in a developing harboring case the government was attempting to make. According to Mrs. Walker, shortly before she rented the Foster Avenue apartment in 1939, she was visiting on the Lower East Side and ran into Emanuel "Mendy" Weiss. She had known Mendy Weiss all her life. When she told Weiss she was out of work, Weiss told her, "I have a proposition for you, and if it works, you will be able to have your rent paid for a year." Weiss told her that he had a friend who was having trouble with his income taxes, that he was a married man, but did not want to be at home should IRS agents want to question or arrest him. Weiss claimed that his friend wanted to take a room, and in a month or two, everything would be straightened out as far as his income-tax problems were concerned. In return for the use of her apartment, this man would pay her rent for one year. Mrs. Walker claimed she did not know the man was Lepke until around June 1939.

Abe Reles told a different story. According to him, Mrs. Walker was in reality a narcotics dealer who worked for Mendy Weiss. Before Lepke was moved to the Foster Avenue apartment, it had been used as a narcotics drop by Weiss, who posed as Mrs. Walker's husband there. Reles claimed that he was positive that Lepke was harbored at Mrs. Walker's apartment from February 1939 until around June 1939 when he was moved to an apartment at 13 Clinton Street in Brooklyn. Not only had Reles visited Lepke at the Foster Avenue address forty or fifty times, he also brought various underworld bosses and hit men there to talk business with Lepke. Among these individuals were Harry Stromberg, aka "Nig Rosen," underworld boss of Philadelphia; Murray Shapiro, a Murder Inc. hit man; Morris "Moey Dimples" Wolensky, a subordinate of Lepke who ran gambling operations in Florida; Albert Anastasia; and Ben "Bugsy" Siegel. Reles claimed that the first time he was taken to the Foster Avenue apartment was by Mendy Weiss, who had a key to the apartment. Reles also stated that he was present when Stromberg visited Lepke, and there was talk about knocking off a witness.

When Weiss first took Reles to see Lepke at the Foster Avenue apartment, he told him that he used the apartment as a drug drop. He also told Reles that Dorothy Walker was okay as she had previously hid out Joey Weiner, a Lepke gunman, at $50 a week. While Lepke was in hiding, he continued to control all contracts and union activities in the garment industry through his minions. Disputes arose regarding Lepke's garment-center rackets. A group of New Jersey mobsters had begun to muscle into some of the garment business. Fearing that he was quietly being pushed aside, Buchalter demanded a meeting with the New Jersey mob regarding his garment-industry interests. Reles personally drove Lepke to the New Jersey sit-down.

Present at the meeting were Abner "Longy" Zwillman; New Jersey mob boss, Willie Moretti; Albert Anastasia; Tommy Lucchese; and others.

Reles testified that Lepke immediately started to dig into the New Jersey mobsters without giving them a chance to tell their side of the story. Lepke complained that because he was away, they were trying to take over his interests. If he were back on the street, they would never try to do it. He told them that he had a vested interest in the garment center for twenty years. Reles later claimed that Lepke stood up and said, "The clothing thing is mine. There is no more argument," and he stormed out of the room. Reles drove him back to his hideout.[17]

Since Lepke had become a fugitive in 1937, he had sensed a wide crack in the foundation of his criminal empire. By late 1937, indictments against Lepke, Louis Kravitz, and other members of the drug-smuggling ring had been handed up. Yasha Katzenberg had been convicted as a principal in the drug operation and given a lighter sentence for turning state's evidence against Lepke.

On August 9, 1937, Special Prosecutor Thomas Dewey presented sufficient evidence for a grand-jury indictment charging the following men with conspiracy to extort money in the flour-trucking, baking, and garment industry: Louis "Lepke" Buchalter; Jacob "Gurrah" Shapiro; Henry Tietlebaum, aka Heinzie (Buchalter's driver and bodyguard); Joseph Miller, Lepke's unwilling partner in the Perfection Coat Front Company; Irving Friedman, aka Danny Fields; Herman Yuran, aka Hymie Yuran; Harry "Big Greenie" Greenberg; Lepke's old strong-arm boss, Sam Weiner; Sam "Red" Levine; Abraham Friedman, aka Yago; Leon Scharf; Joseph Roccabono; Joseph Amoruso, aka "Joe Strawberry" (because of a strawberry-colored birthmark on his face); Paul Berger; and David Hern.

The indictments were being held over the heads of these men as a club to secure testimony against Lepke. These were all men Lepke feared, and the longer he was in hiding, the weaker his influence was over them. Once a single defendant talked and cut a deal, the rest would follow.

Lepke was in a tight spot. Other gangland bosses had gone to jail in similar scenarios, but Lepke did not consider himself like them. He had brains. Buchalter was also suffering from a kidney ailment for which he was regularly treated by a physician. Now he could not get these treatments because the New York police and the F.B.I. were covering doctors' offices and other contact points. In order to convict Lepke, Dewey needed the testimony of a certain group of men. Suppose these men were not around when the trials started? The answer was simple. There wouldn't be any case. They would have to release him.

Lepke always believed in his motto, "No witnesses, no indictments." Eliminating possible witnesses was his only chance. The veneer of a respectable businessman fell from Lepke like a mask. Now he was once again the vicious killer that had worked his way up from the gutters of New York.[18]

According to Harry J. Anslinger, U.S. commissioner of narcotics, "We received word that Lepke had given orders for extermination of all witnesses who could testify against him. Day by day, men would disappear on whom we had counted or the child of an individual who had information would be found dead. The situation with Lepke had become so serious that Thomas E. Dewey, the New York district attorney, called an unprecedented secret meeting of four high-law enforcement officials: F.B.I. Director J. Edgar Hoover, New York Police Commissioner Lewis J. Valentine, District Attorney Dewey himself, and I, representing the Bureau of Narcotics. 'If the killing off of witnesses continues,' Dewey told us, 'there will soon be no one left to testify when we finally catch up with Lepke.'"[19]

It was Lepke's paranoia, which seemed to grow worse with every day he remained on the lam, that in the end brought about his destruction. His obsessive drive to eliminate witnesses forced many underworld characters into the arms of the police to save themselves from a Lepke gunman's bullet. Lepke sent some of his personal staff out of town to keep them safe from Dewey's reach until a particular trial or investigation was over. Potential witnesses close to Lepke were dispersed to various points west of the Mississippi. For witnesses that were uncooperative, Lepke decreed death.

Max Rubin, a lieutenant of Lepke's and very close to the boss, was a good example. For years, the former schoolteacher served as a Lepke aide. Rubin specialized in the garment and trucking part of Lepke's rackets. When Dewey began his investigation as special prosecutor into the garment and baking-industry rackets, Rubin was sent to Salt Lake City, then to the Catskills, and then to New Orleans.

Rubin always became homesick for his wife and children and returned to New York City. Every time that Rubin came home, Lepke became more concerned. The last time Rubin returned to New York, he had been called to Dewey's office. It was reported to Lepke that Rubin, who knew a great deal about the boss's operations, had made lengthy statements to Dewey.

One night, a Lepke gunman picked up Max Rubin and drove him to the corner of Amsterdam Avenue and 150th Street. It was pouring rain that night, and Rubin was ushered into the presence of Lepke, who was standing under an awning. Lepke wanted to know why Rubin came back.

"I get homesick," said Rubin.

"How old are you, Max?" asked Buchalter.

"I'm forty-eight."

"That's a ripe old age," said Buchalter.

A few days later on October 1, 1937, Rubin was walking east on Gunhill Road in the Bronx, returning home. He passed a dark sedan as he neared the corner. A car door opened, and Rubin heard a voice call "Max." He turned his head, there was a flash of flame and a loud report. A slug ripped into his head under his right ear, and he collapsed to the pavement.[20] The bullet entered the back of Rubin's neck, went through his head, and came out between the bridge of his nose and eyes. The nerves of Rubin's neck were severed, the muscles shattered. His head was left permanently crooked.

For thirty-eight days, he lay in the hospital near death, but he lived.[21] His testimony against Lepke was the beginning of the end for the gang leader. The bad aim of the hired killer caused Rubin, now under the protective wing of the D.A.'s office, to become more determined than ever to give evidence against the racket boss. Rubin ended up testifying about Lepke's involvement in the flour and trucking rackets, key testimony that would eventually get Lepke convicted of extortion and sentenced to thirty years to life.[22]

Throughout Lepke's fugitive period, potential witnesses continued to disappear. With law-enforcement pressure growing, by 1939, Lepke had gone on a murder rampage to eliminate anybody who had any connection with his garment rackets, particularly legitimate businessmen who had been forced to submit to Lepke and Gurrah. Aides of Lepke were also fair game. Some of the more high-profile murders took place in 1938 and 1939.

The murder of Hyman Yuran represented a good example of the work of the Brooklyn Combination carry-

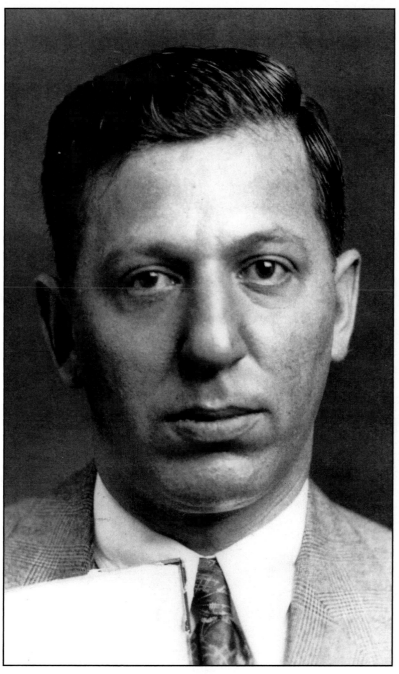

Headshot of Lepke taken June 12, 1933.
(Collections of the Library of Congress)

Lepke sitting in the Federal
Detention Center in Manhattan,
after his August 1939 surrender to J.
Edgar Hoover. (Author's collection)

Above: Mug shot of Lepke taken
June 12, 1933, at the height of
his career as an industrial racketeer. This photo appeared on
one million circulars when he
was a fugitive, 1937-1939.
(Author's collection)

Right: Buchalter arriving at court
for the Rosen murder trial, 1941.
(Library of Congress
Collections)

Thomas E. Dewey during his racket-busting days
as Manhattan special prosecutor, 1935. (Author's
collection)

Sing Sing prison death house photograph of Louis "Lepke"
Buchalter, taken about seven weeks before he went to the
electric chair. (Author's collection)

Sing Sing death house mug shot of Emanuel "Mendy" Weiss. Lepke Lt and a hulking thug. (Author's collection)

Sing Sing death house mug shot of Louis Capone. (Author's collection)

Seymour "Blue Jaw" Magoon, Murder Inc. associate. Magoon was known as "Blue Jaw" because of his always present 5 o'clock shadow. (Author's collection)

Albert "Allie" Tannenbaum, Lepke staff gunman. (Author's collection)

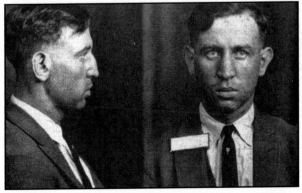

Earliest known mug shot of "Gurrah" Shapiro. (Author's collection)

Harry "Pittsburgh Phil" Strauss, Murder Inc. hit man supreme. (Municipal Archives of the City of New York)

Early mug shot of Louis "Lepke" Buchalter. (Author's collection)

Benjamin "Dopey Benny" Fein. There was nothing dopey about Fein. His sleepy appearance was due to an adenoid condition. (Author's collection)

Left: Manhattan's Garment District, 1936. (Municipal Archives of the City of New York) *Above:* Female garment workers, circa 1920. (Courtesy of the Museum of the City of New York)

Cutters were among the most skilled garment workers. (Author's collection)

Jacob "Little Augie" Orgen. Note the prominent scar on his cheek from an early knife fight. (Author's collection)

Nathan Kaplan aka "Kid Dropper." (Author's collection)

Edward Osterman, better known to history as Monk Eastman. (Collections of the Library of Congress)

Once Lepke became a fugitive his face became very familiar to the public.
(Courtesy *True Detective* magazine)

The body of Albert "Plug" Schuman, a Murder Inc. victim. He was suspected of giving information to the authorities about Lepke and was taken for a ride in 1939. (Municipal Archives of the City of New York)

Left, Captain Cornelius Willemse; and on the right, Louis Kushner aka Cohen. Kushner had just shot Kid Dropper to death. (Author's collection)

Jacob "Gurrah" Shapiro in federal court, 1938. (Collections of the Library of Congress)

Lepke shortly after he surrendered to the Feds in August 1939. Note the mustache and extra body weight. (Collections of the Library of Congress)

Mug shot of Gurrah Shapiro, 1938. (Collections of the Library of Congress)

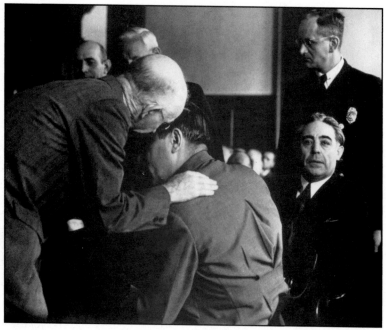

Defense attorney counseling "Mendy" Weiss during the Rosen murder trial in November 1941. Louis Capone is seated behind Weiss. (Collections of the Library of Congress)

Seated far left at table, Lepke Buchalter. Next to Lepke is Mendy Weiss, with his back to the camera. To the right of Weiss is Philip "Little Farvel" Cohen with hand over face and seated next to Cohen is Louis Capone. Taken during jury selection for the Rosen murder trial, August 1941. (Collections of the Library of Congress)

Left: Lepke handcuffed to a deputy U.S. Marshal, on his way to court during the Rosen trial, November 1941. (Collections of the Library of Congress) *Below:* Louis Capone and detective. (Collections of the Library of Congress)

Lepke under heavy guard during one of his many court appearances. (Collections of the Library of Congress)

On the left, Louis Capone and to Capone's right, "Mendy" Weiss handcuffed together on the train to the Sing Sing death house. The man seated behind them is a detective, December 1941. (Collections of the Library of Congress)

Lepke standing in the center between prosecutor and court officer as his death sentence is read to him, December 2, 1941. (Collections of the Library of Congress)

Lepke in good spirits leaving court during his drug smuggling conspiracy trial in 1939. (Collections of the Library of Congress)

$5,000
REWARD

On November 8, 1937, Homer Cummings, Attorney General of the United States, under authority vested in him by law, offered the following rewards:

$2,500 for information furnished to the Federal Bureau of Investigation resulting in the apprehension of **JACOB SHAPIRO;**

$2,500 for information furnished to the Federal Bureau of Investigation resulting in the apprehension of **LOUIS BUCHALTER.**

The photographs and descriptions of the above named persons are hereinafter set out.

Jacob Shapiro was convicted in Federal Court at New York, New York, on November 8, 1936, of violating the Federal Antitrust Laws, and was sentenced to serve two years in a Federal penitentiary and to pay $10,000 fine. On appeal, this conviction was affirmed, and on June 14, 1937, upon his failure to surrender to the United States Marshal, as ordered, his bail in the amount of $10,000 was declared forfeit and a warrant issued for his arrest.

An indictment was returned by the Federal Grand Jury at New York, New York, on November 6, 1933, charging Shapiro and Buchalter, and others, with violating the Federal Antitrust Laws. Both Shapiro and Buchalter failed to appear in Federal Court for trial on July 6, 1937, and bail in the amount of $3,000 for each was forfeited and warrants issued for their arrests on July 7, 1937.

No part of the aforesaid rewards shall be paid to any officials or employees of the Department of Justice. The right is reserved to divide and allocate portions of any of said rewards as between several claimants. The offer provides that all claims to any of the above described rewards and all questions and disputes that may arise as among claimants to the foregoing rewards shall be passed upon by the Attorney General and that his decisions shall be final and conclusive.

Photographs taken February 16, 1936.

JACOB SHAPIRO, with aliases: "GURRAH," CHARLES SHAPIRO, MORRIS FRIEDMAN, SAMUEL DISHOUSE, SAMUEL DISNAHUSEN.

DESCRIPTION: Age, 41 or 42 years (born in Russia about 1895); height, 5' 5½"; weight, 200 lbs.; build, stocky; nationality, Russian, Jewish; hair, medium chestnut; eyes, blue, wears glasses occasionally; complexion, medium - inclined to be flushed; features, large mouth, thick lips, nose somewhat flattened - appearance of having been broken (possibly remodeled by plastic surgery) - large ears; dress, rather conservative - well tailored; speech, very gutteral, Jewish accent; mannerisms, gesticulates with hands when speaking; peculiarities, thick hands and short stubby fingers; fingerprint classification, 11 11 R O 7 Ref: 9, 3, 1 / 26 R I 26 26 26

Photographs taken June 12, 1933.

LOUIS BUCHALTER, with aliases: "LEPKE," LOUIS BUCKHOUSE, LOUIS BUCKHALTER, LOUIS KAWER, LOUIS COHEN, LOUIS BUCKALTER.

DESCRIPTION: Age, 40 years (born February 12, 1897, at New York City); race, white - Jewish; height, 5' 5½"; weight, 160 lbs.; build, medium; hair, dark brown or black; eyes, brown; complexion, dark; peculiarities, nose - large, rather straight and blunt--ears - prominent--eyes - alert and shifting; marital status, married - one son, Harold, aged about 17; fingerprint classification, 25 11 17. / 27 O

Information may be communicated in person, or by telephone or telegraph collect, to the undersigned, or to the nearest office of the Federal Bureau of Investigation, United States Department of Justice, the local addresses and telephone numbers of which are set forth on the reverse side of this notice.

JOHN EDGAR HOOVER, DIRECTOR,
FEDERAL BUREAU OF INVESTIGATION,
UNITED STATES DEPARTMENT OF JUSTICE,
WASHINGTON, D. C.
TELEPHONE, NATIONAL 7117.

November 8, 1937.

The first federal reward circular sent out shortly after Lepke and Gurrah became fugitives in 1937. The amount was later increased to $25,000 to match the reward offered by the City of New York. (Collections of the Library of Congress)

ing out contracts for Lepke against potential witnesses. Yuran was an important Lepke liaison man. Yuran, who was a dress manufacturer, was a missing codefendant with Lepke in the garment-trade racket investigated by D.A. Dewey. He was accused of being a collector and extortionist for Lepke while using his position as a dress manufacturer as a cover. Yuran was first indicted by Dewey when he was special prosecutor in 1937. A broader superceding indictment was returned in January 1939, at which time Yuran was missing.[23]

Abe "Kid Twist" Reles, after becoming a state's witness in 1940, described to the Brooklyn D.A. exactly what had happened to Yuran. He was murdered on July 25, 1938. Yuran was taken for a ride by Harry Strauss, Allie Tannenbaum, and Jack Drucker. These three were widely known Murder Inc. assassins. Yuran was shot several times and thrown face-down into a four-foot grave near a swimming pool drain at the Loch Sheldrake Inn in Loch Sheldrake, Sullivan County. The body was discovered on April 15, 1940, when Sholem Bernstein, an accomplice in the murder, pointed out the location to investigators for the D.A.'s office. Leon Scharf, another Lepke codefendant, disappeared around the same time.[24]

Danny Fields, aka Irving Friedman and Daniel Friedman, had been a loyal aide to Lepke for many years. As a collector and go-between man in Buchalter's garment-center rackets, he knew a lot. Maybe too much for his own good, Lepke thought. Fields was close friends with Louis Kushner, aka Cohen, the killer of Kid Dropper. Cohen had gotten out of prison in 1937 after serving fourteen years for the Dropper murder. Throughout the time he was in prison, Fields visited Cohen, giving him the weekly stipend he had been promised by Lepke.

In December 1938, Fields, who was manager of the Greater New York Tailors Expressman Association, was arrested by detectives of the Grand Jury Squad and brought into custody.[25] Fields was lodged in the Tombs jail when he couldn't raise the $35,000 bail. He was being held as a material witness in Dewey's garment-rackets investigation.

Shortly before Christmas 1938, there appeared in a New York Post gossip column called "The Lyons Den," written by Leonard Lyons, the following item: "Danny Fields, one of Gurrah's co-defendants in the Goldis case [the murder of William Snyder in 1934] is turning state's evidence, a city official assures at the Paradise that's the case upon which Dewey campaigned for D.A."

Shortly thereafter the ex-prize fighter's bail was reduced. The new amount was paid by the Peerless Bonding Company, a Lepke-controlled business, and Fields walked out of the Tombs a free man. The inference was unmistakable. Danny Fields had turned rat, and there was plenty he could tell: forced tribute from merchants and unions; the Lepke mob's weekly payroll; murders, and other crimes of violence he had discussed with Lepke; the racket setup that Lepke controlled.

Lepke had to silence Fields, but how to reach him was a problem. Lepke hit on a solution. Louis Cohen was very chummy with Fields, and he owed Lepke a lot for being carried on the mob's payroll while incarcerated. Lepke sent for Kushner, explaining that Danny Fields was a menace and had to be removed. Still loyal to Lepke, Kushner agreed to act as a lure.

Fields was told by Kushner that Mendy Weiss wanted

to see him. The meeting was supposedly set for late afternoon on January 28, 1939 on Lewis Street on the Lower East Side. At 5:30 P.M., Danny Fields, driving with Kushner sitting next to him in the car, slowed down. "That's the place," Kushner said, pointing to 3 Lewis Street. As soon as Fields stopped the car, Kushner jumped out the passenger side and started to run toward the corner. Fields looked around in surprise. At that instant, two men stepped out of a doorway and fired point-blank. Fields dropped like a log. With cool deliberation, the killers then trained their guns on the running Kushner. Three bullets struck Kushner in the back. Lepke figured it would be just as easy to erase two men as it would be one.

This accounted for two more witnesses who could never testify against Lepke.[26] Conveniently, Weiss had left for a trip to Europe earlier that afternoon and had a perfect alibi. Later information brought out during the Murder Inc. prosecutions in 1940 was that Jacob "Cuppy" Migden, a brother-in-law of Mendy Weiss, was one of the gunmen and Louis Kushner was the other. According to this story, Migden and Kushner were assigned by Weiss to "take" Danny Fields and that Kushner was accidentally killed in the cross fire.[27]

Lepke's next target was Joseph Miller, a retired dress manufacturer who had been indicted along with Lepke and fifteen others for extortion in the garment trades. His connection with the racket dated back to the early thirties when Lepke and Gurrah had muscled into the firm of Miller and Lowe known as the Perfection Coat Front Company and forced Miller, who was the president of the company, to give up a large share of his stock.[28] Up until April 12, 1934 when Miller sold the assets of his firm to a

Samuel Weiner for $30,000, Lepke used the firm's offices as his headquarters.[29] Miller knew and was telling D.A. Dewey about Lepke's systematic shakedown.

At 7:30 P.M. on March 23, 1939, Miller pulled up to the curb in front of his two-family home on West Tremont Avenue. As he was walking toward the entrance of his home, a man seated in the rear of a car behind which Miller had parked called him by name. "Miller, is that you?" he said. Miller, a robust man of fifty, retraced his steps. He saw a partly bald, swarthy man dressed in a black overcoat step out of the car. There was another man sitting behind the wheel. The bald-headed man who called Miller whipped out a pistol and fired at Miller. Miller dove for his assailant and began grappling with him. He twisted the gun from the would-be killer's hand and brought the butt down on his head. The gunman dropped.

By this time, the man behind the wheel joined the fray. Just as Miller struck his confederate, the other gunman opened fire, and Miller toppled to the ground. The driver retrieved the weapon, helped his dazed partner into the car, and sped off. Miller was rushed to the hospital, where seven bullets were extracted from his body. Not a single one of the wounds was serious.

In the would-be assassins' haste, one of them dropped his hat. The hat had a Philadelphia label. (Could this pair have been gunmen sent by Stromberg?) As in the Max Rubin shooting, this bungling was costly. Another fear-driven witness who had escaped death by a hair would testify to the hilt against Lepke.[30]

Abraham "Whitey" Friedman, who had furnished Lepke with gorillas in labor warfare, was now Lepke's codefendant. He was out on $25,000 bail. He had talked with D.A. Dewey about Lepke's dealings with his strong-arm men. He was suspected of telling Dewey more. He was the key figure the D.A. was weaving into an airtight case around Lepke for extortion in the garment-manufacturing industry. Dewey had positive proof that Friedman had collected at least $10,000 in checks from the Lombardi Frock Company. There was no doubt that the stocky ex-con who had risen from the position of strong-arm thug to collector in the Lepke enterprises had taken the money to turn over to the boss. His testimony would give Lepke as a fourth offender a mandatory life sentence.

Lepke ordered Whitey's elimination. In typical fashion, two Murder Inc. car thieves stole the death car. Louis Capone delivered a shotgun and a pistol to be used in the murder several days before Friedman was killed. The shotgun was then cut down by Reles and Harry Strauss with a hacksaw. Another Murder Inc. operative clocked Friedman's coming and going from New York on the train for about a week to find the ideal time when Whitey would be vulnerable.

At first, Reles and Strauss were going to act like detectives and arrest Friedman by flashing phony identification and take him for a one-way ride. They then decided against it because they thought Friedman might resist, and they would have to kill him and his wife at their home.[31]

According to testimony by Reles, Strauss and Seymour "Blue Jaw" Magoon took the shotgun out to the Canarsie section of Brooklyn to try it out. The killers then went to Manhattan to have Friedman pointed out to them. Allie Tannenbaum fingered Friedman for Strauss and Magoon. Magoon and Strauss then followed Friedman onto the subway and rode all the way back to Brooklyn in the same car with him.

On the evening of April 25, 1939, Mikey Syckoff, a Murder Inc. loan shark, saw Friedman getting off the subway at eight o'clock. He then drove by the street where Whitey lived and signaled to Strauss and Magoon, who were sitting in a stolen car. As Syckoff passed the killers, he honked to let them know that Friedman was walking by on his way home. Strauss stepped out of the car behind Friedman and fired one blast from the shotgun into the back of Friedman's head. Whitey dropped, and Strauss jumped into the getaway car, which sped off.[32] One by one, significant witnesses against Lepke were being eliminated.

Lepke was finding it difficult to keep up with the Dewey investigation. He got a tip that his partner in the trucking racket, Morris Diamond, was talking to Dewey. Diamond was office manager of Local 138 of the Teamsters union, the same local whose president, William Snyder, was murdered by Lepke in 1934. Diamond, a 240-pound, slow-moving man of forty-nine, had been subpoenaed by the D.A. as a witness in the garment-center extortion investigation. He had appeared before Dewey on several occasions, and it was reported that he was cooperating fully with the D.A.'s office.[33] Mendy Weiss brought this information to Lepke, who then told Weiss to see Albert Anastasia.[34]

Mendy Weiss picked up Albert Tannenbaum and took him to talk to Anastasia at his Brooklyn hangout. Anastasia introduced him to Jack Parisi, another syndicate killer, and told Tannenbaum to make a date with Parisi for the following day to point out someone. Weiss and

Tannenbaum then drove to Manhattan to meet another man, who pointed out Diamond to Tannenbaum as Diamond came out of Local 138 offices. The next day, Tannenbaum identified Diamond to Parisi. Upon later questioning by the Brooklyn D.A.'s office, Assistant Prosecutor Burton Turkus asked about the conversation that Tannenbaum had with Weiss after Tannenbaum had been shown Diamond.

Turkus: What was said?

Tannenbaum: When I got over to Clinton Street and Broome, Mendy asked me if I saw Diamond. I said, "Yes, I seen him okay." He said, "Tomorrow you meet Jack and point Diamond out to him." Then I asked Mendy, "Who is this fellow? What is it all about?" He said, "Oh, it's just some official connected with the flour bakers, and he is going down to Dewey and giving information about Lepke.

Turkus: When you asked Mendy Weiss what it was all about did you ask him what was going to happen to Morris Diamond?

Tannenbaum: He told me he was going to kill him.[35]

On July 25, 1939, the racket czar's lethal finger pointed at Philip Orlovsky. In the early thirties, a faction of Local No. 4 of the Cutters Union split from the Amalgamated Clothing Workers of America and formed a rival union with the support of the Gorilla Boys' mob. Lepke and Gurrah helped in the recruiting of members, and soon fifteen thousand workers were members of the new union known as the International Clothing Workers.

The new union formed its first and largest local in Vineland, New Jersey, the location of a large vest factory operated by Nathan Borish, a close business associate of Lepke's. The racket czar had made him dummy president of his Raleigh Garment Company. In the battle between Sidney Hillman, president of the Amalgamated Clothing Workers, and Lepke, Orlovsky had been used as a pawn.

When the struggle to recruit members for the new union was going on, Lepke diverted his support of Orlovsky's faction when he was offered a monopoly in the trucking of clothing between New York and New Jersey and took advantage of it by becoming owner of Garfield Express. It was reported that Lepke received a $300,000 cash settlement to end the rift between the Amalgamated and the rival union. With Lepke's support withdrawn, the rival union collapsed.[36] Orlovsky, as a result, had no affection for Lepke and when brought in front of a grand jury, told the entire story.

Philip Orlovsky's slaying was planned for July 25, 1939. Seymour "Blue Jaw" Magoon, Abe Levine, and Martin "Buggsy" Goldstein, Reles's erstwhile partner, were given the contract. On the morning of July 21, 1939, Magoon and Goldstein stole a blue 1939 Pontiac model sedan.[37] A garage attendant later identified all three men as the ones who stole the car.[38] At approximately 6:00 A.M. on July 25, the blue Pontiac driven by Magoon with Goldstein as the gunman pulled to the curb about a block from Orlovsky's Brooklyn apartment. Fifteen minutes later, Irving Penn, an executive in the music-publishing house of G. Schirmer, left his apartment and began his daily walk to the subway to go to his office. He was short, but weighed 200 pounds, and he had the terrible misfortune of closely resembling Orlovsky, who lived in the same apartment building.

As Penn walked by the car, Goldstein stepped out onto the running board and fired six shots into Penn. Penn collapsed and died three hours later in a local hospital. When questioned by detectives in his brief lapses of consciousness, he claimed that he had no idea why someone would want to murder him. Police later found the stolen car and a .32-caliber pistol. The Penn slayers had mistaken him for Philip Orlovsky. Seymour Magoon would cut a deal with the prosecutor in the Penn slaying and become a state's witness.

The accidental murder of Penn, a legitimate businessman, put even-more heat on the underworld. Lepke was moved into the position of national Public Enemy No. 1 by the F.B.I. By the summer of 1939, Buchalter's aides were dwindling. Weiss had become a fugitive as the feds were looking for him on a narcotics-peddling charge. Anastasia began to think that the Foster Avenue address was no longer safe, and arrangements were made to move Lepke to a basement apartment at 13 Third Street in Brooklyn. The building was owned by a Maria Nostra, a friend of Albert Anastasia. Occasionally, Lepke had gone to Maria Nostra's apartment to meet his wife, who was brought there by Louis Capone.[39] There is some evidence that Lepke spent the last month or two as a fugitive in a basement apartment at that address.[40]

In July 1939, about one month before Lepke turned himself in, Anastasia brought him a message from New Jersey. The substance of the message was that Lepke should either turn himself in to the feds or else. Lepke was undecided as to what to do. By this time, other mob leaders felt because of the heat put on the underworld by the Lepke investigation through grand-jury proceedings in the Southern District of New York, other racketeers in the New York metropolitan area might end up being indicted. It would be much better for everybody if Lepke surrendered.

About the middle of July 1939, Mendy Weiss told Lepke that the mob was working on a plan whereby Lepke was supposed to walk in. Asked what kind of a deal he could get, Weiss said that the feds were going to give Lepke twelve years. Lepke wanted no more than eight. According to Weiss, part of the agreed-upon deal was that Lepke would not be turned over to Dewey to face charges on the extortion indictment.

Mendy Weiss later told Abe Reles that if Lepke did not turn himself in, it looked like there might be a gang war, as Lepke had received an ultimatum, walk in or else. According to Weiss, Albert Anastasia brought word to Lepke that a meeting was held at which Abe Zwillman, Moey Dimples, Ben Siegel, Willie Moore, and other Eastern mob bosses were present. Anastasia was called to the meeting as he was Lepke's sponsor. They gave Anastasia a message to give to Lepke. The message was that it would be best for him to turn himself in because the mob could not stand the pressure that was being brought to bear on them.[41]

According to Charles "Lucky" Luciano, who was serving a thirty-to-sixty-year sentence for his 1936 compulsory prostitution conviction by Dewey, he engineered Buchalter's surrender to the feds.

"We couldn't just knock off Lep the way it happened with [Dutch] Schultz. That would just mean more trouble. Hoover would be sore as a boil at anybody stealin' his glory, and Dewey would go through the ceiling. We had to get Lep out of our hair once and for all, but we had to do it in some way that would still give Dewey and Hoover their piece of cake." Luciano claimed he ordered New York and Brooklyn underworld bosses to stop protecting Lepke.

"The way I figured it," Luciano said, "the most-important thing was to make it look to Lep like we'd worked out a deal with Hoover. If he'd give himself up to the F.B.I. and take the narcotics rap, he'd have Hoover's guarantee that he wouldn't be turned over to Dewey, and by the time he'd finished his federal stretch, the Dewey case would probably've caved in. I knew that Lep was scared to death of Tom Dewey especially after what that prick done to me. Of course, we didn't make no deal at all with Hoover, but it had to look damn sure to Lepke that we did."

Luciano also told his lieutenant, Tommy Lucchese, that the plan had to be brought to Lepke by somebody he trusted completely. Morris "Moey Dimples" Wolensky, who had worked in gambling operations for Lansky and Lepke and was a very close friend of Buchalter, was selected for the job. Wolensky was dispatched as an intermediary completely unaware that he was leading Lepke into a trap. Two years underground with mounting pressures and tensions of hiding out had made Lepke compliant enough to be willing to accept what seemed reasonable terms.

At the beginning of August 1939, word reached Luciano of Lepke's compliance on condition that he surrender to J. Edgar Hoover personally and that Albert Anastasia drive him to that meeting. According to Luciano, Frank Costello, his second in command, made a deal with *New York Daily Mirror* gossip columnist Walter Winchell to make arrangements for Lepke's surrender with Hoover. Winchell and Hoover were good friends. Luciano claimed that the arrangement was made not only to make Hoover look good, but to gain favor with Dewey.[42]

There may be some truth in Luciano's statements. Yet it seems highly unlikely that Lepke would have agreed to any edict that did not come from the full board of governors of the underworld. A manhunt for Buchalter was going full blast. The heat was on in the underworld. Racket operations would remain locked up tight until this Lepke thing was settled.

Naturally, a tremendous amount of advice was pouring in from Lepke's close associates. As underworld business was hurt more and more, sentiment seemed to go in one direction. Lepke should surrender before underworld operations were ruined. After all, there was the temptation of a $50,000 reward. One of his own men might turn him in, or worse, kill him to collect it. Lepke was suspicious of the motives of most of his former associates. Now Lepke's own friends and business associates were putting the heat on. Lepke knew the credo of the syndicate that no one man matters against the well-being of the organization as a whole. The ever-increasing counsel to give up was only a lightly disguised decree. If he did not surrender, he would be hit.

Now aside from his personal bodyguard, Abe Reles, Lepke felt he could only rely on Albert Anastasia and Moey "Dimples" Wolensky, his longtime friend and lieutenant. One day, Dimples was sent to Lepke's hideout.

Wolensky had been duped into presenting a surrender deal to Lepke. He dropped a blockbuster into Lepke's indecision and uncertainty. He told Lepke that a deal had been arranged with the feds. According to Wolensky, he had been picked to bring Lepke the word because very few visitors were permitted to the hideout anymore. Wolensky told Lepke that the deal had been approved. He was to surrender to the F.B.I. and answer only to the narcotics violations with a maximum sentence of ten to twelve years. The phony deal was a rope thrown to a drowning man in Lepke's mind.

Interestingly, Anastasia consistently argued to Lepke against his surrender. This seems to be proof that Luciano issued no edict to underworld bosses regarding the protection of Lepke. If an ultimatum had been issued from Joe Adonis or Costello dictated on the command of the F.B.I. or otherwise, Anastasia never would have been against Lepke's surrender or continued to protect Lepke.

Lepke respected Anastasia throughout his months in hiding. He had proved to Lepke that he could trust him with his life. On the other hand, the deal presented to Lepke by Wolensky seemed to remove all risk of falling into the hands of the state just as Luciano had predicted. This changed the situation for Lepke. Believing Wolensky's pitch to be true, he agreed to surrender to J. Edgar Hoover personally. It appears that this decision was made entirely by Lepke himself based on false information.[43]

An agreement was made with Walter Winchell, the New York gossip columnist, that Lepke would only surrender to J. Edgar Hoover. Winchell set up all the arrangements with Hoover, and a meeting place was arranged in

Manhattan. At 10:17 P.M. August 24, 1939, Lepke was driven to Twenty-eighth Street and Fifth Avenue by Albert Anastasia. The car was parked behind Hoover's, and Lepke was quickly escorted to Hoover's car.[44] According to Winchell, he introduced Lepke to Hoover.

"'Mr. Hoover,' we said, 'This is Lepke.' 'How do you do?' said Mr. Hoover, affably. 'Glad to meet you,' replied Lepke. 'Let's go.' 'To the Federal Building at Foley Square,' Hoover ordered the driver."[45]

Many years afterward, Lepke told a friend that it felt like a ton of bricks had hit him. From the F.B.I. chief's very first words, Lepke realized that there was no deal. Not Hoover, not Winchell, nor had the Department of Justice been a party to any deal. Dimples had double-crossed him, he thought. "I wanted to get out of the car again as soon as I heard, only I couldn't," said Lepke.[46]

There was one brief final touch to the story of the hired hand who had double-crossed the boss. In 1943, there was a shootout in a mid-Manhattan restaurant. When the smoke cleared, Dimples was dead. Lepke was in prison then with little chance of ever getting out. A friend brought Lepke the news of Dimples's demise. "You know," reported the friend, "when Louis heard that Dimples got it, I never saw him look happier. I always thought Dimples was his pal."[47]

Once Lepke was in custody, Hoover made arrangements for him to have a short visit with his wife and stepson. Shortly after, Lepke was booked, fingerprinted, and photographed. He had $1,700 in cash in his pocket. He gave $1,100 to his stepson and $600 to the jailer for expenses.[48] The feds wanted Lepke on two indictments: violation of the narcotics laws and the old indictment charging racketeering in the fur industry and violation of the Sherman Antitrust law.[49]

On August 25, 1939, Lepke was arraigned before Judge Samuel Mandelbaum in federal court. He pleaded not guilty to ten indictments charging that he smuggled narcotics into the country in 1935 and 1936 and that he committed various acts of bribery in paying off customs officials. He was also indicted twice by New York County grand juries for garment-center and baking-industry extortion.[50]

In the meantime, friction between the feds and Thomas Dewey's office was growing. Dewey's assistants were denied access to Lepke. The government stated that Lepke was a federal prisoner, and while every reasonable cooperation would be extended to the county D.A.'s office, the federal charges would have to be disposed of first.[51]

On September 2, 1939, Emanuel "Mendy" Weiss, Lepke's key lieutenant, was arrested on a charge of conspiring to bring narcotics into the country from Canada. He was also wanted for questioning in the murders of Danny Fields and Louis Cohen.[52] On November 6, 1939, five people were found guilty of aiding Lepke when he was a fugitive. They were all officials of the Raleigh Manufacturing Company, which was making payments indirectly to Lepke of $250 a week while he was in hiding. The government charged that the weekly payments shown on the books of the Baltimore corporation were sent to Lepke and Gurrah. This was considered a test case of the federal law against harboring fugitives.[53]

On November 3, 1939, a superceding indictment containing eighteen counts of extortion and attempted extortion in the flour-trucking racket was handed up by a New York County grand jury against Max Silverman,

Harold Silverman, Sam Schorr, and two unnamed persons, one of whom was Lepke. The previous indictment was handed up when Dewey was still a special prosecutor in 1937. It named Gurrah, Lepke, Max and Harold Silverman, and Schorr. Gurrah was not named in the new indictment.[54]

While Lepke was awaiting trial on the drug-smuggling charges, witnesses continued to be eliminated. Big Harry Greenberg had been sent out of town by Lepke when the Dewey investigation began. Greenberg was in charge of Lepke's strong-arm goons in the early thirties and knew a lot about the boss' operations. For years, Greenberg had been an insider in dealings with the needle trades. With the beginning of the Dewey probe, Greenberg went on the lam to Canada. Soon he was running out of money.

In the spring of 1939, he wrote Lepke from Montreal for additional funds. His letter sounded threatening. He wrote, "I hope you guys are not forgetting me, you better not."

At this time, Lepke was in hiding and eliminating witnesses as fast as they were being called to Dewey's office. To Mendy Weiss, Greenie's letter was ominous. Like Mendy, the rest of the gang interpreted the letter as an ultimatum. Greenberg was given the death penalty.

At first, Allie Tannenbaum was ordered to Montreal to do the job. Tannenbaum went north and set up a watch across from Greenberg's hideout. Even before Allie arrived, Greenberg was gone. In the next few weeks, Greenberg was racing with death. He ended up in California and was living in a rented Hollywood house.[55]

Ben "Bugsy" Siegel visited Lepke at his Foster Avenue

hideout in Brooklyn, and the matter of Greenberg was discussed. Attempts on Greenberg's life failed in Montreal and later Detroit. Now, Lepke had received word that Greenberg was living at the Hollywood address. Siegel told Lepke that if Greenberg was there, he would take care of the murder. As was always the case with Murder Inc. assassins, the job was well planned. A few days prior to the actual murder, Sidney "Shimmy" Salles, a Lepke gunman later to become a statistic himself, came to Allie Tannenbaum's home in Brooklyn and informed him that he was to go to California the next day, but not to say anything about it to anybody.

The following morning, Tannenbaum met Salles at a hotel as was previously arranged. Tannenbaum was then driven to the Newark, New Jersey, airport where he met New Jersey crime boss Abner "Longy" Zwillman and his lieutenant, Jerry Catena. Zwillman gave Tannenbaum a package containing two guns and $250, with instructions to go to Philadelphia and there purchase cartridges for the guns and an airplane ticket for Los Angeles. Tannenbaum followed through on the instruction and took a plane at Camden, New Jersey, for the coast.

In L.A., Tannenbaum was met by Frankie Carbo, an underworld fight promoter and New York mobster who was invited by Siegel to participate in the murder of Greenberg. Tannenbaum was driven to Carbo's apartment. After about an hour, Siegel came in, and Tannenbaum turned over to Siegel the two guns he had carried to the coast.[56]

The murder was planned for the night of November 22, 1939.[57] On that night, Siegel, Carbo, and Tannenbaum rode in Siegel's automobile to Hollywood where a stolen car had been left in readiness for them. Carbo and Siegel then entered the stolen car, which was driven by Siegel, while Tannenbaum drove Siegel's car and followed them to where Greenberg lived. There they waited for Greenberg to return home. Siegel stayed in the stolen car. Tannenbaum remained in Siegel's car, and Carbo waited in the street directly opposite Greenberg's home.[58]

Shortly afterward, Greenberg, who had gone out to pick up a newspaper, pulled into the driveway. Carbo walked up to the side of Greenberg's car and emptied his pistol into Greenberg. The deadly assault was so sudden that Greenberg was taken completely by surprise. Carbo fired the pistol at almost point-blank range. Two bullets went through Greenberg's right shoulder and two more tore through his head. The pistol had been so close that there were powder burns on Greenberg's face.[59]

After the shooting, Carbo jumped back into the stolen car driven by Siegel. Closely followed by Tannenbaum in Siegel's car, they drove a distance of several blocks. There the stolen car was abandoned. Another car was also waiting where the stolen car was left. This car was driven by a friend of Siegel's known as "Champ" Segal. Champ was instructed by Bugsy to drive Tannenbaum to San Francisco where Tannenbaum was instructed to board a plane and return to New York.

It has never been explained why Ben Siegel took a personal role in the sidewalk execution of Big Greenie. He had asked for an Eastern gunman, and Tannenbaum had been handpicked for the job. Big Greenie was a small-time sinner who didn't merit that kind of attention from a syndicate boss. Perhaps Siegel, who had not been involved in a syndicate disciplinary action for several years, felt that he needed a personal killing to emphasize his continuing authority.[60]

Another potential witness was eliminated, but the biggest surprise for Lepke was yet to come.

10 Trials and Tribulations

"The smuggling of narcotics deserves stern punishment. The leaders of the gangs in violating Federal laws prey on the moral and physical fiber of their victims in dealing with habit forming drugs that eventually destroy addicts."[1]

In December 1939, Lepke went on trial in U.S. federal court on the drug-smuggling charges that had been pending against him since 1937. Most of his coconspirators had been tried, convicted, and sentenced while Lepke was a fugitive. These codefendants included Jacob "Yasha" Katzenberg, who had agreed to testify against Lepke in return for a lesser sentence.

One of the first witnesses to take the stand against Lepke was a tough mobster who had feigned allegiance to Lepke and then went home at night to keep books on the accused gangster's $10-million international narcotics-smuggling racket. In reality, he was a federal agent. Al Kearns, the undercover man, sat at the side of Assistant U.S. Attorney Martin as the prosecutor outlined the methods by which the $10-million worth of narcotics were imported into the country between 1935 and 1937. Martin explained how the gigantic ring bought narcotics in China and shipped them via Marseilles, Bordeaux, and

Cherbourg. The drugs originated in Tientsin, China, from a factory supposedly operated by Chinese army officers.

It was told how Lepke made no specific agreement with Katzenberg, but just muscled into the smuggling ring. "That's my connection you're using," Buchalter was quoted as saying to Katzenberg. Katzenberg agreed. "I want my share," Buchalter demanded. He first put himself down for 60 percent and later settled for 50 percent. The importing system worked smoothly with the help of a Japanese doctor on one end, two Greek businessmen in the middle, and Customs Inspector John McAdams at the Port of New York providing the necessary customs stamps.[2]

Mr. Martin, in an hour-and-a-half recital of the syndicate's operations, conceded that Lepke, who until then had restricted himself to large-scale industrial rackets, wanted no part of the narcotics racket at first. It was only after the ring successfully smuggled its first trunkload of narcotics into the country, with its own members slapping customs stamps on the trunks, that Lepke became interested. Then, according to Mr. Martin, Lepke went to Katzenberg and demanded his cut.

So that there would be no question as to what constituted 50 percent of a shipment, Lepke arranged that half of each shipment brought into the country by the couriers was to be turned over immediately upon arrival to a Lepke lieutenant named Louis Kravitz. Kravitz was named as a defendant in the indictment, but at that time was a fugitive.

According to testimony, the ring had two sources of supply in China. One source was an illicit drug factory in a Shanghai airplane hangar. The other source was a Dr.

Santsuki of Kobe, Japan, whose price list was reported to contain every variety of opiates known to man. Once the couriers arrived in Shanghai, they would contact the drug ring's representative through a Greek family who lived there.

The syndicate sent attractive women or respectable-looking men to Shanghai to meet the ring's representative. There, one or two trunks would be loaded with narcotics for each traveler. The presumed tourists would then travel to France where they would be met by the ring's resident agent. The agent would accompany the courier to New York on an ocean liner, and members of the drug ring would meet the agent and courier on the pier.

More details of the operation were revealed, how by bribing customs agents, the syndicate acquired the necessary customs stamps, how trunks would be passed by a member of the smuggling ring, who would slap the necessary customs stamp on each trunk. The jury was told about the two trunks loaded with narcotics that were hijacked. Customs Sgt. John McAdams, who had pleaded guilty to being an employee of the smuggling ring, was suspected of having something to do with the hijacking. McAdams was promptly visited by a member of the smuggling ring who warned him of Lepke's interest in the narcotics. The trunks would have to be returned unless McAdams wanted to be killed by the Lepke mob. The trunks were never returned, but McAdams lived.[3]

One of the first witnesses to take the stand against Lepke was a courier named Nate Gross. Gross had been involved in the actual smuggling operation. The bulk of Gross's testimony had to do with his trips to China as a courier for the drug ring. According to Gross, Katzenberg made the initial proposal to him about taking a trip to China. Nate Gross and another defendant named Sam Gross (no relation to Nate) were told that their trip would be fully paid. The two Grosses received $8,000 to go to Seattle where they met another representative of the ring and were given an additional $4,000. Sam Gross then directed Nate to forward $6,000 to Shanghai under his own name. According to Nate Gross, when he arrived in China, he would cash the U.S. funds into Chinese currency. The narcotics that he purchased were reported to have originated in Tientsin, China. He would then travel the same route explained by Assistant U.S. Attorney Martin back to the U.S.[4]

On December 7, 1939, Jacob "Yasha" Katzenberg finally faced Lepke on the witness stand. Katzenberg was brought from Leavenworth Prison where he was serving his ten-year sentence on the drug-smuggling conviction. Katzenberg explained to the court that in the Orient, the couriers bought thirty-seven kilograms of narcotics at $240 per kilogram on each trip. They were then shipped back to New York.[5]

Katzenberg's testimony differed somewhat from his original trial testimony regarding Lepke. He had originally stated that he had gone to Lepke to try to interest him in getting involved in the smuggling operation. In that testimony, Katzenberg said it was Lepke who made the arrangements to bribe U.S. customs officials in order to get the necessary stamps. Lepke had also set up the original contacts in Shanghai. During Katzenberg's trial, it appeared that he and Lepke had agreed upon the specifics of the drug-smuggling operation. Now he claimed that Lepke had muscled in after setting up the contacts.

During the second week of the trial, two more witnesses linked Lepke with the smuggling ring. Stella Williams, a courier on the fourth shipment, identified Lepke as the boss of the operation. Former customs officer John McAdams also identified Lepke with the operation. McAdams told the court that he was paid $1,000 a trip for looking the other way. He explained that he had gotten into the racket by agreeing to pass the trunks full of what he thought were watch movements. McAdams claimed that even after accepting his share for the first five shipments, he did not know that they were narcotics.[6]

As Lepke's narcotics trial was in progress, another potential Lepke witness was found in a shallow grave near Folsom, New Jersey. Irving Mandel, a professional gambler with connections to Lepke, had been stabbed then shot to death. For more than fifteen months, the feds had sought Mandel for questioning in the Lepke case. Mandel had been stabbed twice in the back and shot through the temple.[7]

As 4:05 P.M. on December 13, 1939, the government completed its case against Lepke in the court of Judge John C. Knox. At this time, Lepke lieutenant Louis Kravitz, who was a fugitive, was described as a sort of general business manager for Lepke and the narcotics ring, the man who sold to wholesalers and controlled prices and percentages.[8]

Confident that the government had failed to prove that Lepke was the leader of the narcotics-smuggling ring, Lepke's attorney, William W. Kleinman, asked the jury in his summation to consider his client as the defendant and not as Lepke. He began his argument with the plea that the jurors disregard the "Lepke myth."

Mr. Kleinman eloquently said, "A verdict reached just because he is Lepke would constitute a breach of fundamental American traditions. It would be putting a wedge into the dike which keeps the sea of chaos from the land of law and order.

"But I know what is on your minds because there isn't a person who lives in the city of New York who hasn't heard stories about Lepke, hasn't read them, hasn't discussed them. You can't tell me that there hasn't been some moment at which you have thought, 'Oh well, this is a prosecution against Lepke, what difference does it make, the end justifies the means?' Yet such an attitude constitutes a violation not only of the juror's oath, but [breaks] a high law. The law of doing justice. You must give him the same kind of a square deal and a fair trial that each of you would expect in his place. I am not making any comparison, but there is only one brand of justice and he is entitled to that. Nothing more, nothing less!"[9]

The narcotics-conspiracy trial ended at 10:47 P.M. December 20, 1939. Despite Mr. Kleinman's speech, a jury of eight women and four men convicted Louis "Lepke" Buchalter and his codefendant, Max Schmuckler, of conspiracy to violate the narcotics laws. A third defendant, David Kardunick, was acquitted. This case was considered the most-important narcotics case tried in federal court up to that time. Lepke expected the verdict and did not bat an eye when the verdict was read to the court. Judge Knox commended the jury on what he called a righteous verdict. The court set January 2, 1940, as the date for sentencing. Lepke believed that with the federal conviction he would be safe from the clutches of Thomas E. Dewey.[10]

On January 2, 1940, Lepke was sentenced to a total of fourteen years. The sentence was broken down as follows: two years for the narcotics-conspiracy conviction, two years for the racket antitrust conviction (originally in the 1936 indictment), ten years for the narcotics-smuggling conviction, and ten years probation. Lepke would have to serve his federal sentence before any state sentence was imposed.

Lepke was shipped to New York City to stand trial for extortion in the baking, garment, and flour-trucking industries. D.A. Thomas E. Dewey had accepted the terms laid down by Attorney General Frank Murphy for the granting of a writ of habeas corpus. Lepke was scheduled to stand trial on the extortion charges with his old partners, Max and Harold Silverman, Sam Schorr, and William "Wolfie" Goldis.[11]

The extortion case against Lepke and his former partners would represent the climax of Thomas Dewey's gangbusting career. Lepke and his codefendants were accused in a blanket indictment of conducting the bakery and flour-trucking rackets during the course of which William Snyder, president of Teamsters Local 138, was murdered. In a separate indictment, Lepke and his partner, Gurrah Shapiro, were charged with extortion in the garment industry.[12]

The office of the U.S. Attorney for the Southern District of New York, John T. Cahill, agreed on January 3, 1940, to an order directing the U.S. Marshal's Office to produce Lepke before Judge John J. Freschi in General Sessions Court in New York City on January 4, 1940, at 10:00 A.M. for arraignment on the indictment charging Lepke and four codefendants with extortion and attempted extortion in the New York City baking and flour-trucking industry.

The U.S. Attorney's consent to a writ of habeas corpus signed by Judge Freschi cleared the way for Lepke's trial in the state of New York on the bakery-racket indictment, as well as a similar indictment charging racketeering in the garment industry. (Note: A writ of habeas corpus is an order requiring that a prisoner be brought before a judge or into court to decide whether he or she is held lawfully.) The surrender of Lepke to the New York County D.A.'s office followed an autographed request from Thomas Dewey to Attorney General Frank Murphy after Lepke's sentencing on the drug-smuggling conviction in U.S. district court.

In accordance with the writ, Lepke would remain in the Federal House of Detention in Manhattan during his trial and would be produced in General Sessions Court by U.S. marshals for his arraignment and for each day of the resulting trials. Upon completion of the New York State trials and after sentencing in General Sessions Court, he would be sent back to the federal penitentiary to serve the fourteen-year term imposed on him by federal Judge Knox in U.S. district court. Upon completion of his federal sentence, he would be turned over to state authorities.[13]

On the advice of his lawyers, Lepke stood mute on the twenty-three-count extortion and attempted extortion indictment in General Sessions Court on January 4. A plea of not guilty was entered into the record.[14] On January 6, it was learned that a superceding indictment made possible by additional testimony from witnesses who were afraid to come forward while Lepke was still at large was to be returned by a grand jury within a few days. The true bill would take the place of a previous indictment handed down in 1937. The new indictment was reported to contain fifty counts of extortion in the garment industry.[15] Lepke's attorneys argued that Dewey's effort to place Lepke on trial in the state of New York was illegal because he was a federal ward, and therefore, the order of the General Sessions Court signed by Judge Freschi directing Lepke to appear for trial was worthless.[16]

On January 6, Lepke lost his fight to keep out of state court when federal Judge Bondy, after hearing an extended argument by Lepke's attorneys, dismissed a writ of habeas corpus issued January 5, 1940, by U.S. Judge Holbert, which would have prevented Lepke's appearance in state court.[17]

On January 17, 1940, it was announced in General Sessions Court that the sum of $514,000 involved in the garment-industry extortion racket and listed in the indictment against Lepke, Gurrah, and others was the largest amount ever contained in a United States indictment. D.A. Thomas Dewey disclosed that all four garment industries in New York City were infested with racketeers. These included men's clothing, women's garments, sponging or the treating of cloth, and trucking. Crimes ranging from mayhem to murder were alleged to have been perpetrated by Lepke and his partners to extort money from the industry.[18]

Lepke, Shapiro, and seven others were named in the superseding indictment charging thirty-six counts of extortion and attempted extortion in the garment industry. The indictment was based on a four-and-a-half-year investigation by Dewey and Assistant D.A.s Gurfein and Herwitz. It described an alleged extortion racket five times larger than any revealed in the city of New York's history. Each count of the indictment named a firm said to have been victimized by the Lepke mob. Dewey's office had withheld the names of the firms for fear that Lepke's organization might seek to silence the victims with threats. According to Dewey's office, at least six murders had grown out of this racket. Alleged extortions totaled $514,000 in the indictment, but Dewey estimated the true amount to be in the many millions of dollars.[19]

On January 24, 1940, the trial of Louis "Lepke" Buchalter and his codefendants opened in General Sessions Court. This first trial was for extortion in the baking and flour-trucking industry. The trial was halted on a note of unexpected and intense excitement before it actually got underway. William "Wolfie" Goldis, former president of Teamsters Local 138 Flour Trucking Union, arose and pleaded guilty to each of the counts of the indictment.

Lepke was shocked. Beet red, he turned around and in a sneering tone whispered to Goldis, "You dirty rat!" It was obvious to everyone present in the courtroom that Lepke was livid and extremely agitated. He pounded the table in front of him and appeared dazed. It was now obvious that Goldis stood as the state's principal witness against Lepke and the codefendants.[20] Obviously, a deal had been cut with Goldis, who was under indictment for the murder of William Snyder. Goldis offered to plead guilty to a manslaughter charge in the fall of 1939 in return for his testimony against Lepke in the baking and flour-trucking extortion racket.[21]

On February 2, 1940, Aaron Held, the flour trucker who had the courage to stand up to the Lepke mob, told the court how he had paid thousands of dollars to Lepke and his gang to save his business. Held stated that he had been trucking flour to New York City bakers since 1916 and never had any trouble until Lepke came along in 1930. After that, Held's life became a nightmare with strike after strike endangering his business and the ever-increasing demands of Lepke and his mob. He pointed out to the court Lepke, Max Silverman, whom he described as Lepke's chief aide, and Sam Schorr, a former labor organizer. Held claimed that Silverman and Schorr were collectors of Lepke's share of the industries' toll.

Held described how he first met Lepke in 1930 when he was considering a merger with another trucking company. Held claimed that even after he yielded to Lepke and joined the racketeer-controlled Flour Truckmen's Association, he was continually taxed with additional fees, which by the end of 1935, had grown to $225 a week. Held claimed that the racketeers became so arrogant that when he was called to come up with an unexpected $2,500 assessment and only had $500, Schorr refused to take the cash on account.[22]

It was like Lepke's former partners and codefendants were rats leaving a sinking ship. On February 7, 1940, Lepke and the defense received another blow. Louis Solomon, legal counsel for Sam Schorr, former business agent of Local 138, got up and stated to the court that his client wished to plead guilty on all counts of the indictment. Solomon added that Schorr would be available as a witness if the D.A. wanted him to testify. Schorr's plea left only Lepke and Max and Harold Silverman to stand trial on the extortion charges.[23]

Another Lepke aide was back to haunt the gang leader.

On February 13, 1940, Max Rubin, the Lepke lieutenant who had been shot in the head and miraculously lived, testified that William Solomon, an influential Tammany Hall district leader, received 10 percent of a $15,000 shakedown of a baking concern. According to Rubin, the agreement was negotiated in Solomon's office in 1935. Rubin explained to the jury that in the spring of 1935, he gave Solomon $1,000 from the shakedown and six months later gave him another $500. Rubin testified that Max Silverman engineered the shakedown when he thought that the Lepke mob could extort $25,000 from the Gottfried Baking Company by making a move to organize its employees.

Rubin said the idea was first opposed by William "Wolfie" Goldis and Sam Schorr as too dangerous. Lepke, however, approved the scheme. Employees of the Gottfried Baking Company were given circulars and then called out on strike. After an unsuccessful attempt to obtain $25,000 from the company to end the strike through an intermediary, Rubin visited Solomon's office with Lepke for a meeting with Samuel Miller, the director of Gottfried Baking Company, to try to "straighten him out."

According to Rubin, Miller had exasperated Lepke by turning in complaints to the D.A.'s office and to officials in Washington. Rubin stated that the Tammany Hall leader introduced him and Lepke to Miller. Lepke refused to shake Miller's hand. Lepke then talked to Solomon in the corner, and Rubin talked to Miller, assuring him that had he known that the baking company official was a friend of Solomon's, there would have been no strike at Gottfried.

Miller then offered $15,000 to have the strike called off because it was ruining the company's business. Rubin claimed that he had Lepke's okay to settle the strike at any price. Rubin immediately agreed to the $15,000. Rubin stated, "We agreed that Miller was to pay $10,000 in two days and $5,000 in six months. I got $10,000 a few days later in Billy Solomon's office. I turned over $1,000 to Solomon and brought $9,000 to Lepke."[24]

Of the $9,000 he brought to Lepke, Rubin remembered the gang boss taking $4,000 and giving the other $5,000 to be divided up between Goldis and Schorr.[25]

D.A. Thomas E. Dewey wasted no time. On February 14, 1940, Tammany district leader William Solomon was indicted for extortion, bribery, and taking unlawful fees. This indictment was described as the worst blow to the New York City Democratic political machine since the Jimmy Hines case. Hines, a district leader, had been convicted of taking money from the Dutch Schultz mob to protect the Harlem numbers racket.[26]

Miller testified that he paid $15,000 to Rubin to get relief from the strike called by Lepke. The exchange was made in the offices of William Solomon, Seventeenth Assembly district leader. Miller told how he had pleaded with both state and federal authorities for help before paying the extortion money. With no relief forthcoming, he had to bow to Lepke's demands. Miller testified that the actual amount paid to Lepke's representatives was $20,000. According to Miller, $5,000 had been paid to Max Silverman before the negotiations with Lepke to do something about easing the labor trouble.[27]

On February 17, 1940, the state rested its case against Lepke and the two Silvermans. This was shortly after witnesses for the state told of two more shakedowns by Lepke and his codefendants. David Lasner, former president of the Flour Truckmen's Association and the owner of a large trucking concern, testified that in 1935 he gave Max Silverman $15,000 to stop the interference of labor-union gorillas with drivers of Dugan Brothers. Lasner said he paid the money in two installments. Abraham J. Levy, vice president of the Henry S. Levy Baking Company, testified that in 1935 he paid the Lepke mob $1,500 to call off a strike of his drivers. Witness after witness gave devastating testimony against Lepke and his gang.[28]

On March 2, 1940, Lepke and his two codefendants were convicted on charges of extortion in the bakery and flour-trucking rackets. Lepke was found guilty on fifteen counts of the indictment. He was, as a result, condemned to state prison for a life term as a fourth felony offender. Max and Harold Silverman were also convicted on fifteen counts.[29]

The jury delivered its guilty verdict at 1:24 A.M. March 2 after deliberating for thirteen hours and thirty-nine minutes. The case was in court for thirty-nine days. On April 6, 1940, Lepke was sentenced to thirty years to life. Max Silverman was sentenced to a term of twenty to thirty years, and Harold Silverman a term of three to six years.[30]

For becoming state witnesses, the Goldis brothers got off with light terms. William "Wolfie" Goldis was sentenced to a year and a half for his part in the 1934 murder of William Snyder. Morris Goldis, the admitted slayer of Snyder, was allowed to plead guilty on a first-degree manslaughter charge and sentenced to five to eight years in prison. Morris Goldis pleaded guilty on February 4, 1941.

Assistant D.A. Grumet argued that Morris and Wolfie Goldis were forced to do the murder. If they hadn't, they, too, would have been killed.[31]

By this time, Lepke had to assume that he would be spending the rest of his life in prison. Shipped back to Leavenworth after being prosecuted and convicted of extortion charges by Dewey, he probably began to feel at ease. The biggest surprise was yet to come with the Murder Inc. prosecutions in 1940. By the time Lepke was sentenced on the extortion conviction, Abe Reles had begun to talk to the Brooklyn prosecutor about murders in the New York City area. He also began to talk about Lepke's connection to some of these murders.

11 Murder 1

"I stood enough of this crap. That son of a bitch Rosen, that bastard he's going around and shooting off his mouth about seeing Dewey. He and nobody else is going any place and doing any talking. I'll take care of him."[1]
—Louis "Lepke" Buchalter, September 11, 1936

At approximately 6:50 A.M. on September 13, 1936, Louis Stamler went to wake up his son to go to work when gunfire shattered the morning stillness of his Brownsville, Brooklyn, neighborhood. Stamler ran to the window of his Sutter Avenue apartment just in time to see a black, two-door sedan with four men in it speed away from the front of a candy store at 725 Sutter Avenue and disappear.

Stamler got dressed and ran down to the candy store to find Joe Rosen, the owner of the establishment, lying flat on his back on the floor in a growing pool of blood.[2] Stamler yelled for a policeman who happened to be putting on signal lights on Sutter Avenue. Patrolman Guglielmo Cappadora of the Seventy-fifth Precinct ran down to the candy store where he saw Rosen's body. He quickly checked to see if Rosen was still alive. There was no pulse. He asked Stamler if he knew who did it or if he had seen a car. Stamler gave the officer the license number, which Cappadora sent out over the air from the Seventy-fifth Precinct.[3]

Rosen was declared dead on arrival at the hospital. He was forty-six years old and had $29 in his pocket. It was obvious that this was no holdup, but beyond that the police did not have a clue as to the motive for the murder or who the gunmen were.[4] For almost four years, the murder of Joseph Rosen remained a mystery, the homicide case unsolved.

By April 1940, Lepke was back in his cell in Leavenworth where he assumed that he would spend the remainder of his fourteen-year federal sentence for narcotics smuggling. Then, on March 22, 1940, the bombshell hit. Abe "Kid Twist" Reles, the leader of the Brownsville gang that was a part of the Brooklyn Combination had cut a deal with the law.

It will be remembered that Reles and the Brownsville mob had personal dealings with Lepke. Reles had also served as Lepke's contact man and personal bodyguard during the two years that the gang leader was a fugitive. Now, in return for leniency in the form of immunity from prosecution, Reles agreed to tell Brooklyn D.A. William O'Dwyer everything that he knew about organized crime. The information divulged by Abe Reles was some of the most-significant testimony that has ever been disclosed about the structure and day-to-day operations of organized crime, both in the New York area and on the national arena.

This was long before the law-enforcement community had any knowledge of the scope and power of organized crime in the United States. Reles was the first significant organized crime figure to come forward. This was years before mob turncoats such as Joe Valachi, Henry Hill, and Sammy "Bull" Gravano told their stories.

As a midlevel boss, Reles handled the murder contracts and the day-to-day business of the Brownsville mob. He knew the people who had gotten hit and why the contracts had been handed down. More important than this, Reles knew where the necessary corroboration for the murder cases could be found. According to Section 399 of the New York State Criminal Code for 1940: "A conviction cannot be had upon the testimony of an accomplice unless he is corroborated by such other evidence as tends to connect the defendant with the commission of the crime." In New York, an informer could accuse an accomplice of a felony, and there could never be a conviction unless evidence was forthcoming from a nonaccomplice.[5]

When Reles began to talk to the D.A. about various unsolved Brooklyn murders, he mentioned a contract to take Joseph Rosen, a former trucker and candy-store operator, who had been shot to death in his Sutter Avenue candy store in 1936. Sources close to O'Dwyer told the media that he planned to take legal action against the imprisoned Lepke as the result of information he had received about a homicide.[6]

Reles told the D.A. that sometime in May 1939, he had met Mendy Weiss on the corner of Saratoga and Livonia avenues in Brooklyn. Weiss was looking for Harry "Pittsburgh Phil" Strauss to talk to him about a murder contract they were working on. When Reles told Weiss that Strauss was not around, Weiss replied, "He [Strauss] must be crazy. On the Rosen job, after I killed the guy, he kept on shooting and making unnecessary noise."[7] At this point,

Reles was told about the Rosen contract, who was involved, and why.

In May 1940, indictments came out against Louis "Lepke" Buchalter, Harry "Pittsburgh Phil" Strauss, Louis Capone, Emanuel "Mendy" Weiss, James Feracco, and Philip "Little Farvel" Cohen charging them with first-degree murder in the death of Joseph Rosen on September 13, 1936. O'Dwyer told the press that Cohen and Feracco were fugitives and Weiss was on bail as a defendant in a pending narcotics case. He was soon to be a fugitive. Capone was described as the liaison officer for the Brooklyn rackets and was being held as a material witness on a $100,000 bail.[8] Rosen, who had been put out of his trucking business by Lepke and his mob in 1932, was threatening to go down and talk to D.A. Dewey about Lepke's machinations.

Max Rubin, the Lepke operative who had been shot in the head in 1937 and miraculously lived, would be a key witness for the prosecution in the Rosen murder case. Rubin had testified against Lepke in the flour-trucking and garment-industry racket trials in 1937 and 1939. Rubin never mentioned the Rosen murder when he was questioned by Assistant D.A. William E. McCarthy in 1937. He admitted knowing Rosen and even implied that Mendy Weiss might have been involved, but would say no more.

Rubin had been implicated in the Rosen murder in 1936 in an article that appeared in the *New York Post*. He was not named, but the article read: "An official of a clothing drivers union and a former business associate were connected with the murder of Joseph Rosen."[9]

On December 16, 1937, Assistant D.A. William E.

McCarthy, who was working with Special Prosecutor Dewey, talked with Max Rubin. McCarthy said, "We want to question you about the Joseph Rosen murder. Of course, you know you were over to the Joseph Rosen store—that's before the grand jury now. Even if it does involve you, we are not going to prosecute you." Max Rubin replied, "I was only over to the store once, and that was on an invitation from Louis Feinberg, from the union I represent."

Asked by the assistant D.A. if he knew anything at all about the murder, Rubin replied, "No." Rubin continued, "I want to tell you something, McCarthy. They shot me, those bastards, and if I knew how to bury them, I would do it."[10] Rubin had lied. He was willing to testify against Lepke in the extortion cases, but was terrified of the power of the boss. This was especially true at the time because Lepke was a fugitive and had been conducting his murder rampage against potential witnesses.

Persuading Rubin to talk about the Rosen murder even once his old boss was in custody was almost impossible. He could not believe that the Brooklyn D.A. was really serious about prosecuting Lepke on the old murder. According to Assistant Brooklyn D.A. Burton Turkus, "Only after five or six weeks of every argument we could offer would he even accept the fact that we were serious about trying Lepke." An assistant D.A. could offer him immunity from prosecution, but not from Lepke and his mob.

When Rubin finally agreed to testify in the 1941 murder trial, Kings County Judge Franklin Taylor asked him to explain why he had perjured himself in front of a grand jury some three-and-a-half years before. Rubin charged that Lepke had pipelines even into the grand-jury room.

"I went to the grand jury where no one knew I was, and I was shot in the head." Had he given a true statement, Rubin felt that it would have been death to himself and his family.[11]

Max Rubin's testimony was very significant. In order to obtain a murder conviction against Lepke, it would be necessary to have someone as a state's witness that was very close to the boss. In order to understand Lepke's connection to the Joseph Rosen murder, it is important to review the background of Max Rubin. Rubin became an executive board member and one of the finance committee of Local No. 4 of the Cutters Union of the Amalgamated Clothing Workers of America. As an official of the Amalgamated, Rubin came to know Lepke intimately and was with him almost daily. He also worked for Lepke in connection with Local 138 of the Flour Truckmen's Union and the Greater New York Tailors Expressmen's Association. Later, Rubin became business agent of Local 240 of the Clothing Drivers and Helpers Union, which was affiliated with the Amalgamated.

In 1931, a dispute arose between two groups in Local No. 4 of the Amalgamated. Lepke supported one group, which gained control. Rubin arranged a meeting between the leader of the opposing group and Lepke, and certain officials were given a year's pay and withdrew from the union. Rubin was kept on by Lepke as business agent of Local 240. Rubin was present at the meeting at which it was arranged by a general organizer for Amalgamated that Danny Fields (murdered by a Lepke execution squad in 1939) and Paul Berger (the finger man in the Rosen murder) were made intermediaries between the Amalgamated and Lepke.

In 1932, Lepke told Rubin that the union wished a stoppage on a specified date of all the trucks that carted clothing in and out of New York City. Rubin told Lepke that he believed he could stop all the trucks except those of three concerns: Garfield Express Company, Branch Storage, and the New York and New Jersey Transportation Company (the company in which Joe Rosen was a partner). Rosen's operation handled both union and nonunion work. The Garfield Express Company, owned by Louis Cooper and located in Passaic, New Jersey, was nonunion and operated in competition with New York and New Jersey Company in Passaic. New York and New Jersey Company did business in New York and New Jersey and had a little business in Pennsylvania. Lepke said that the Pennsylvania business had to be given up.

Rubin visited the New York and New Jersey Company officers, then returned and told Lepke that when he told Rosen that he would have to give up the Pennsylvania business, Rosen told him that it was the only thing he had in the business. Rosen had no money invested in the New York and New Jersey Company. It was the Pennsylvania business that he brought in that allowed him to become a partner in the trucking company. Rosen's two other associates also objected. Lepke was a 50-percent owner in the Garfield Express Company. It would be to his advantage to eliminate the New York and New Jersey Transportation Company.

Lepke told Rubin that he wanted to see Rosen, and they met in the office of one of Lepke's former business associates. At this meeting, Rosen explained to Lepke that the Pennsylvania business was the only thing he had in the New York and New Jersey Company and that if he lost that, he would lose everything. Lepke asked to see his books. Also present at this meeting were Danny Fields and Lepke's partner, Gurrah.[12]

In response to a telephone call, Rosen's books were brought up to the meeting by his daughter, Sylvia Rosen, who was also his bookkeeper.[13] When questioned shortly after her father's murder, Sylvia Rosen said in her deposition, "They told him that he could not go on. That he would have to get out of the business."[14] Rosen said he would be ruined. Rubin told him "not to hit his head against a stone wall." Lepke then promised Rosen that they would do something for him.

The stoppage occurred, and Rosen was forced out of the New York and New Jersey Company. The Garfield Express Company profited materially as a result. Later, Rubin had a talk with Rosen in which Rosen complained that everyone else had returned to work after the stoppage, but that he was still "on the street." When Rubin reported this to Lepke, he asked what could be done for Rosen. Rubin suggested that Rosen had once worked for Garfield Express as a foreman. Maybe Louis Cooper might hire him back. Lepke arranged for Rosen to go to work for Garfield Express.

About eight months later, Cooper fired Rosen and refused requests from Rubin and Lepke to take him back.[15] In a statement taken in the D.A.'s office in December 1937, Rubin told an assistant D.A. why Rosen was fired. At this time, Rubin said he had the one and only conversation he ever had with Esther Rosen, Joe's widow. "I met her once when her husband was fired from Larry Cooper's job stealing hams. She pleaded with me to go over to Larry Cooper's, which I did, and I tried to get him to be reinstated, but I couldn't do it. Cooper took the position that he didn't care what he did with the manufacturers, but when he robbed from him, that was enough."[16] Rosen was then out of work for sixteen months during which period he complained to Rubin that he was a married man with a family and that they had nothing to eat.

After the appointment of Thomas E. Dewey as special prosecutor, Rubin told Buchalter that they had a desperate man on their hands, that they had to get him a job, that he was doing too much talking, and that they were likely to get into a lot of trouble, but that Rosen was willing to work for anything. Lepke arranged to get Rosen a job as a driver. Rosen had to quit after a short time because he was having heart trouble. On borrowed funds, Rosen opened a little candy store on Sutter Avenue in Brooklyn in the spring of 1936.[17]

In June 1936, Lepke told Rubin that Rosen was going around Brownsville "shooting off his mouth that he is going down to Dewey's office." Rubin told Buchalter that he would get the members of Local 240 to patronize Rosen's store. Lepke didn't care what Rubin did so long as Rosen kept quiet. Rubin then called a meeting of the Local 240 executive board and arranged for local members to spend money in Rosen's store.

In July, Lepke again told Rubin that Rosen was threatening to go down to Dewey's office. Rubin assured Lepke that there was nothing to worry about, that Rosen must be up against it. Later, Sylvia Rosen Greenspan, Rosen's daughter, asked Rubin if he would visit her father. Rubin told Lepke that this would be a good opportunity to straighten out Rosen. Lepke ordered Rubin to give Rosen $200 and to tell him to stay out of town until he was told to return. Rubin gave the money to Rosen, and Rosen said he would go to his son's home in Reading, Pennsylvania.[18]

The next time Lepke spoke to Rubin was on Friday, September 11, 1936. Lepke was angry when Rubin walked into the office. It was the first time he had ever seen the gang leader in a rage. Lepke claimed that Rosen had only stayed out of town a few days and had double-crossed him. "I had no more than walked in," Rubin recalled later, "when Lepke was yelling, his face was flushed." "I stood enough of this crap," he quoted Lepke as yelling. "That son of a bitch Rosen, that bastard, he's going around and shooting off his mouth about seeing Dewey. He and nobody else is going any place and doing any talking."[19]

Rubin begged Lepke not to be rash and to remember that he (Rubin) had visited Rosen's store in July and to let him handle the problem. Rubin made another attempt to get Rosen a job, but union officials said they could do nothing. Rubin returned and told Lepke what had transpired. Lepke then directed Rubin to get Paul Berger right away. Rubin found Berger and told him that Lepke wanted to see him. Rubin then left to attend a union ball game in Vineland, New Jersey. He stayed in Atlantic City until Sunday afternoon, September 13, 1936.[20]

Paul Berger was Lepke's intermediary with the Cutters Union and a former strong-arm man. Lepke directed Berger to point out Joe Rosen to somebody. Lepke and Berger then took a taxi downtown and met Mendy Weiss. Lepke directed Berger to go with Mendy to Brooklyn looking for Joe Rosen. They drove to Brooklyn in Mendy's car, and Berger, who had known Rosen from business transactions, identified him to Weiss. They also stopped for a moment to talk to Louis Capone on a Brownsville street corner. The murder contract was set into motion. Within forty-eight hours after Lepke sent for Berger, Rosen was murdered.

The specifics were later described by Sholem Bernstein, a shylock and car thief who did business with the Brooklyn Combination. Sholem was scheduled by the mob for death in early 1940 after it was decided that he knew too much. By April 1940, Sholem was arrested and held on a $25,000 bond as a material witness in the Murder Inc. investigation. His arrest probably saved his life. After talking with mob turncoat Abe Reles, Bernstein agreed to become a state's witness.[21] Rosen's murder contract was carried out with Murder Inc. precision.

By Bernstein's account, a few days prior to September 13, 1936, Harry Strauss met him at the corner of Sackman and Livonia avenues in Brooklyn. Bernstein was sitting in his parked car. Harry Strauss came along and got in. While they were talking, Louis Capone, Mendy Weiss, and Philip "Little Farvel" Cohen walked up. They called Strauss, who got out of Bernstein's car and walked over to Mendy's vehicle. Capone, Cohen, Strauss, and Mendy got into the car, where they sat for about an hour talking.

At the end of their conversation, Strauss walked back to Bernstein's car and ordered him to steal a car and get a "drop." (A drop was a private garage that was usually rented for a month and used as a place to hide the stolen car until it was used on a particular job.) According to Bernstein, at about three the next morning, he and a friend, another car thief named Harry "Muggsy" Cohen, stole a black, two-door Chevrolet sedan from the area of Lafferts and Empire Boulevard in Brooklyn. Cohen broke the window and started the car with a "hot box" (a jump box to start the ignition when you haven't got the ignition key). The two men then drove the car to Lincoln Place and Ralph where Bernstein had rented a private garage earlier that day. Once the men pulled the car inside, they left for the night.

The next morning, Cohen and Bernstein went back to the drop and took the handle from the car and brought it to a locksmith to have a key made. The door-handle key fit the ignition. Cohen took the radio out of the car in anticipation of selling it later. This was his pay for helping Bernstein steal the car.

The following day, Bernstein went back to the corner of Sackman and Livonia and told Strauss that he had the car. Louis Capone was with Strauss. When Mendy Weiss had stopped to talk to Capone several days earlier, it was Capone who put the wheels in motion for the Rosen murder contract.

Capone wanted Bernstein to go through the getaway route with him, which he did seven or eight times. They drove by Rosen's candy store, at which time Capone told him, "We are going to kill somebody in this candy store." Bernstein was to be the getaway-car driver. When Capone and Bernstein returned to the corner, Strauss ordered Bernstein to go out and steal license plates to put on the stolen car. Later he stole a set of plates off a car in a locked garage in East Flatbush. Bernstein then returned to the drop and put the plates on the stolen car. The original plates were broken up and disposed of.

Bernstein was told by Strauss to bring the stolen car to the "corner" at 11:00 P.M. on September 12, 1936. When Bernstein got there, Mendy Weiss, Harry Strauss, Louis Capone, Farvel Cohen, and Jimmie Ferracco were waiting. Harry Strauss told a man named Joe Pilch to bring the guns for the Rosen job over to the car. Pilch brought the guns, which were wrapped in a package, and gave them to Strauss, who put them in the glove box of the stolen car. Then Bernstein was told to drive the car to Bradford and Blake streets and meet them in a little park there. Bernstein waited a few minutes at the designated place. Weiss, Strauss, Cohen, and Feracco came over. Capone was not with them. Weiss told the group, "I am going over to the store and see how everything is," meaning is it clear to kill Rosen.

Weiss was gone about a half hour. When he returned, he asked Harry Strauss to come back with him. The two were gone about fifteen more minutes. Strauss didn't like the situation. There were too many people in and around the store, and he was afraid he might be recognized. Weiss said to the group that "we will return in the morning." Strauss told Bernstein to take the car back to the private garage. Then he returned to Farvel Cohen's apartment.

Bernstein spent the night there with Strauss, Cohen, Mendy Weiss, and Feracco. At 5:00 A.M. September 13, 1936, they woke up Bernstein and told him to get the stolen car and bring it back to the park. Later, Mendy, Strauss, and Feracco came along. They decided to go into a hallway on Wyona Street and Blake Avenue and wait. This was across the street from where Joe Rosen lived and around the corner from his candy store.

Strauss told Bernstein to bring the package in the glove box containing the guns. The package was opened, and three revolvers were taken out. Strauss gave a gun to Mendy, a gun to Feracco, and kept one for himself. The men stayed in the hallway about forty-five minutes. Weiss then saw Rosen come out of the house and followed him. Weiss came back and told the others he saw Rosen open the store.

Strauss told Bernstein to take the stolen car and pull it up in front of the candy store. Bernstein pulled the car around and stopped in front of Rosen's store with the motor running. Weiss, Strauss, and Feracco started walking towards the building. Weiss and Strauss went in, and Feracco stayed outside as a lookout. Bernstein said he heard a number of shots before the three men piled into the car and they took off. Bernstein drove the gunmen to Van Sinderin and Livonia avenues about fourteen blocks from Rosen's candy store. The four men abandoned the stolen car at this point and walked over a bridge that crossed the BMT tracks and led down to Junius Street on the other side of the bridge.

Louis Capone, driving Bernstein's car, and Farvel Cohen, in another vehicle, waited to take the gunmen away. Capone got out of Bernstein's car and told him to take Feracco to the station. Mendy offered to give Bernstein his gun, but Bernstein refused. Weiss then gave the revolver to Feracco. Bernstein drove off in his car with Feracco, and Capone, Strauss, and Weiss drove away in Farvel Cohen's car.

Bernstein took the gun that Weiss gave to Feracco and later broke it up with a hammer and threw the parts down a sewer. When he was questioned by the assistant D.A., he was asked, "Will you tell us why you did that [drove the car]?" Bernstein replied, "On account of fear of being killed." "Of whom were you afraid?" asked the D.A. "Of Harry Strauss and the rest of the Combination over there." "Ever have any reason to kill Rosen?" asked the D.A.

"Never knew his name until I saw the paper the next day," replied Bernstein.[22] Because Bernstein had business dealings with the Combination, he was expected to go on various jobs with the group.

In the spring of 1940, with Abe Reles, Sholem Bernstein, Allie Tannenbaum, Seymour Magoon, and other Murder Inc. gunmen turning state's evidence, one indictment followed another. On May 28, 1940, D.A. William O'Dwyer conferred with Harold Kennedy, U.S. Attorney for the Southern District of New York, to discuss ways and means by which Lepke could be turned over to Kings County authorities to face the Rosen murder indictment. At this time, Phillip "Little Farvel" Cohen, Mendy Weiss, and James Feracco were fugitives. Strauss, who was being tried on another murder charge, and Louis Capone were arraigned that same day on the Rosen murder charge.[23]

On September 20, 1940, O'Dwyer flew to Washington to arrange for the transfer of Lepke from Leavenworth to face the first-degree murder indictment.[24] On November 30, 1940, Phillip Cohen was arrested in Brooklyn.[25]

In January 1941, O'Dwyer, accompanied by Acting New York Police Department Capt. Frank Bals, traveled to Leavenworth to see if they could cut a deal with Lepke. If he agreed to tell all he knew about Murder Inc. and the underworld in general, he would escape prosecution in connection with the murder of Joseph Rosen. This was the second time law-enforcement officials offered Lepke immunity from prosecution in return for his testimony. When Captain Bals visited the first time in the fall of 1940, Lepke said, "Tell O'Dwyer he can go to hell!" Since his first visit to Lepke, more evidence in the Rosen murder had been obtained. This new information shoved Lepke closer to the electric chair, and it was hoped that as a result he would be willing to talk.[26]

While waiting trial in the Rosen murder, Farvel Cohen was given ten years on a morphine-peddling conviction. Cohen and three associates had developed a scheme for chemically swelling the drug and selling it for double the price. The group was found guilty on federal charges of concealment of narcotics and conspiracy to produce and sell morphine.[27] Cohen was later severed from the Joe Rosen murder case because of lack of evidence. He spent the next eight years in federal prison on the federal narcotics conviction. On September 16, 1949, Cohen's body was found in Valley Stream, Long Island, with six bullets in his head.[28] Whether it was old enemies who caught up with Farvel or new ones was never learned.

On February 7, 1941, another potential Lepke witness, Benjamin "Benny the Boss" Tannenbaum, was eliminated as he baby-sat for a friend in a Bronx apartment. Tannenbaum was a Lepke strong-arm man who was on the mob's payroll for years. Evidently, Tannenbaum put up a terrific struggle with the gunman. A lamp in the apartment had been knocked over and smashed, a table overturned, and the rug was scuffed up and heavily stained.[29] His slayer had evidently emptied a pistol at Benny. Two bullets had pierced his chest. Two penetrated the apartment wall, and the other went wild. There was a bad bruise on Tannenbaum's head, apparently inflicted by a blackjack found on the floor.[30]

It was believed that Benny knew too much about three murders. According to Murder Inc. informer Seymour "Blue Jaw" Magoon, Tannenbaum assisted Charlie "the

Bug" Workman, a Lepke staff killer, on several murder contracts. At the time, Tannenbaum was under indictment in the 1937 Walter Sage murder case. Sage was a slot-machine operator who worked for the Brooklyn Combination.[31]

In April 1941, Mendy Weiss was arrested by federal agents in Kansas City. He had been a fugitive for more than a year after jumping bail while awaiting a federal narcotics indictment. Farvel Cohen and three others had already been convicted on the narcotics charge. Brooklyn D.A. O'Dwyer conferred with U.S. Attorney Harold M. Kennedy on whether Weiss should be tried first in the Rosen murder case or on the narcotics charge.[32]

On April 17, 1941, another potential Lepke witness was shot to death. Sidney "Shimmy" Salles, an aide to Benny Siegel, was reported to know a lot about the murder of former Lepke underling Big Greenie Greenberg, who was shot to death in Los Angeles in 1939.[33] Salles was on the lam at the time of his murder. Police had been looking for him on suspicion of having harbored Lepke when he was a fugitive.[34]

On April 29, 1941, a writ of habeas corpus was signed by Kings County Judge Franklin Taylor in Brooklyn directing federal authorities to produce Lepke in Brooklyn on May 9, 1941, for arraignment in the Rosen murder.[35] On that date, Lepke appeared in Kings County court surrounded by thirty New York Police Department officers and detectives, twelve deputy sheriffs, and five assistant U.S. marshals. Shocked at this entourage, county Judge George W. Martin berated authorities. "This is ridiculous," the judge said. "Why don't you send down to Fort Dix for a company of marines and to the police department for a riot squad? The place looks like an arsenal. We don't need all of you here. We can take care of this ourselves."

Lepke seemed nervous as he faced the court. "I have just arrived from Leavenworth," he said, "and have not had time to retain counsel. I would like permission to see my people and talk to them about getting a lawyer." The judge approved a week's adjournment.[36]

In June, Lepke's attorney filed a plea that Lepke be permitted to stay in Leavenworth prison for the rest of his federal narcotics sentence. Buchalter indicated his desire on June 10, 1941, in an application for a writ of habeas corpus.[37] An affidavit that revealed for the first time the evidence on which Brooklyn D.A. O'Dwyer based the Rosen murder charge against Lepke was presented before federal Judge John Cox to answer the writ of habeas corpus. The defense argued that as a federal prisoner, Lepke could not be turned over to the state. The legal wrangling continued.[38]

On June 19, Louis Capone's attorneys made application for Capone to be given a separate trial. Capone claimed through his attorney that a jury would be prejudiced if he went to trial together with Lepke, whom defense attorneys described as a notorious police character. The court pointed out that it was the contention of the Brooklyn D.A.'s office that members of the Combination received their schooling in crime from Capone and that Capone was in fact a partner with Reles, Strauss, and others in their racket schemes. County Judge Peter J. Brancato denied the application for a separate trial.[39]

D.A. O'Dwyer's insistence that Lepke be tried on the Rosen murder charge was upheld on June 19, 1941 by federal Judge Edward A. Conger.[40] Buchalter was scheduled to go on trial with Weiss, Capone, and Cohen on August 4, 1941. Next, defense attorneys attempted to get a change of venue for the trial, stating that the defendants could not get a fair trial in Brooklyn. The change-of-venue request was also denied.

On August 4, 1941, jury selection began in the Kings County courtroom of Judge Franklin Taylor. Two-hundred-fifty jurors were called for potential service. By the end of the day, 129 had sought to avoid jury duty for various reasons. The defendants were Lepke, Mendy Weiss, Louis Capone, and Philip Cohen.[41] The Rosen murder trial was postponed on August 15 until September 15, 1941, because of the number of potential jurors who did not want to serve.[42]

On September 15, 1941, the Rosen murder trial again opened in Brooklyn. At this point, Philip "Little Farvel" Cohen was granted severance from the trial during the morning session. The prosecutor's evidence against Cohen was lacking.[43] It took a full five weeks to pick a jury for the Lepke trial and twenty-two court sessions, several of which ran into the night. The jury of twelve men and two alternates was finally completed on October 17. It was the longest time required to pick a jury in Kings County and probably the longest in the state up until that time.[44]

On October 20, 1941, the prosecution opened the trial with Assistant Prosecutor Burton Turkus disclosing that Max Rubin, Lepke's old lieutenant, would finger him in the Rosen murder. Turkus charged that Lepke, his chief aide, Emanuel "Mendy" Weiss, and Louis Capone conspired to kill Rosen. Turkus charged that at the time, Rosen was a potential witness against Lepke's racket activities and that Lepke had ordered a war of extermination against all witnesses.

Turkus continued, saying that Max Rubin would testify that Lepke had given him $200 to give Rosen with instructions that Rosen leave town. When Rosen returned and demanded more money, Lepke ruled that he was to be murdered. Turkus explained how Rosen was driven out of the trucking business by Lepke in 1933 and that later Max Rubin had incurred the displeasure of Lepke and was shot in the head. Rubin recovered and agreed to testify for the prosecution.

Turkus then told of how Weiss and Harry "Pittsburgh Phil" Strauss had visited Rosen's store the night before the murder and studied the location for the best way to kill Rosen and then get away from the scene. Weiss and Strauss were the actual killers of Joe Rosen, Turkus explained to the court.

Turkus described how the two gunmen shot Rosen to death and how they were assisted in their escape by Capone and two other underworld associates. One, Jimmie Feracco, was a fugitive at the time of the trial, and the other, Sholem Bernstein, was a witness for the prosecution.[45]

The testimony of the first witness for the prosecution caused a sensation. Esther Rosen, Joe's wife, got up and pointed out Mendy Weiss as the man she had seen in the candy store the day before the murder. "Saturday night I seen some fellow. Now that he [Joe Rosen] was killed Sunday, some fellow walked in Saturday night, but when I saw the fellow's picture, I identified the fellow. He walked in and bought a single cigarette. He was looking behind the counter, I thought nothing of it."[46]

On October 23, 1941, Rosen's son, Harold, testified that Lepke was the man he saw conferring with his father in the lobby of Manhattan's Broadway Central Hotel in 1933. He had driven his father to the meeting with Lepke. He said that the conference started in a hotel room upstairs and ended in the lobby.[47] Rosen described how he had watched Lepke hold an animated conversation with his father during which "Lepke pushed his face within six inches of my father's face."

Harold Rosen's testimony was designed by the prosecution to support Turkus's contention that Rosen was driven out of business by Lepke and later slain because he was a potential witness before Thomas E. Dewey concerning Lepke's rackets.[48] During a deposition taken by the D.A.'s office shortly after the murder of Joseph Rosen, an assistant D.A. had asked Harold Rosen, "Is it your impression and your conclusion that the motive for the killing of your father was to prevent him from telling Dewey about the practices of Lepke, Gurrah, or any other men?" Harold Rosen replied, "That is it. I can't see any other motive."[49]

Hirsch Merlis, another prosecution witness, described how on the morning of September 13, 1936, he was arranging newspapers at his father's stand at Livonia and Van Sinderin avenues when an automobile came roaring off Livonia onto Van Sinderin and pulled to a stop with the brakes screeching. Four men jumped out, ran over a footbridge crossing a railroad cut nearby, and disappeared onto Junius Street. It was the prosecution's contention that the four men, Weiss, Strauss (executed in June 1941 for another murder conviction), Jimmie Feracco, and Sholem Bernstein, were fleeing from the Rosen murder scene.[50] Bernstein was soon to testify for the prosecution.

The incriminating testimony against Lepke and his subordinates kept flooding into the courtroom. On October 23, 1941, Mrs. Sylvia Rosen Greenspan, Joseph Rosen's bookkeeper daughter, testified. She told the court how she had received a telephone call from her father one day in the summer of 1932 asking her to bring his trucking firm's books downtown to an office. Sylvia brought the books to one of Lepke's offices where she saw Max Rubin, Lepke, Danny Fields, and Shapiro. She described how Shapiro studied the ledgers. Lepke, hovering behind Shapiro, would stoop over and whisper in his ear from time to time. She said that Shapiro read off various names of clothing firms on the ledger with which Joe Rosen was told he could not do business.

She said, "My father became very excited, and he said he doesn't see why he should do it. If the manufacturers wanted to give him work, he could not see why he could not have it since he was doing a legitimate business. My father was very excited. He was very pale. Then Max Rubin advised my father to take what he could get."[51] Lepke, as part of his defense, had said that he never met Joe Rosen's daughter. Sylvia Rosen Greenspan corroborated Max Rubin's story by saying that she met Lepke and saw him and her father together before his death.[52]

On October 24, 1941, Sholem Bernstein, the car thief, shylock, and getaway car driver in the Rosen murder, took the stand and described in detail the planning and execution of the job. When asked by Assistant Prosecutor Turkus if he did many jobs for Louis Capone, without telling what they were, Bernstein answered, "Many times." Bernstein described how he was ordered to steal the car just before the murder and how Louis Capone bawled him out for stealing a two-door rather than a four-door car (four doors are easier to get in and out of quickly).[53] Pressed by defense attorneys as to whether he was an informer, Bernstein replied, "All right, I am a stool pigeon, otherwise a rat. Does that satisfy you, counselor?"

Bernstein described how he had stolen about seventy-five cars for the Brooklyn Combination over the years. He also described how he waited in the getaway car while Weiss, Harry "Pittsburgh Phil" Strauss, and Feracco got out. Weiss and Strauss entered the store while Feracco remained outside as a lookout. He also explained how after Rosen was murdered the gunmen piled into the car that Bernstein drove fourteen blocks to rendezvous with Louis Capone and Farvel Cohen, who were waiting in two cars to take the gunmen away from the area.[54]

Bernstein told the court that he thought the job was going to be a "schlammin." When asked by defense attorneys what "schlammin" meant, Bernstein replied, "It means breaking someone's head with a lead pipe." Bernstein continued that he would not have let his friend, Muggsy Cohen, steal the radio from the stolen car had he known the car would be used in a murder.[55] Bernstein later went back and retrieved the radio from Cohen, busted it up, and disposed of the parts.

On October 31, 1941, another star witness for the prosecution took the stand. Lepke's close lieutenant, Max Rubin, explained Lepke's activities in the Amalgamated Clothing Workers of America. Depicting himself as a sort of liaison man for Lepke, he told how his boss had driven Joseph Rosen out of business and how Lepke became angry and profane when he heard that Rosen was threatening to expose the racketeer before Thomas E. Dewey in 1936. He described how he had pleaded with Lepke to spare Rosen only to learn two days later that Rosen had been murdered. Rubin told the court that Lepke ordered him to hide out after Rosen was killed because William McCarthy, then an assistant D.A. in Brooklyn, was working hard on the case and had threatened to collar Lepke.[56]

Frequently, while giving testimony, Rubin would glance at Lepke with a smug grin. Asked by defense counsel if he had done any slugging or strong-arm work for the union, Rubin turned toward Lepke and held up his hands and said, "They're too small. I had to use my mouth as an organizer."[57] When asked by Lepke counsel Hyman Barshay about his earlier story that after the Rosen killing he told Lepke he was in trouble, Rubin cried, "I was in tremendous trouble. I thought the world would cave in on me!" "Was your conscience bothering you?" Barshay asked. "Was your conscience bothering you?" Rubin snapped. "I won't roll in the gutter with you," Barshay said. Trembling with rage, Rubin rose from his seat and shouted, "I rolled in the gutter with a bullet in my head."[58]

On November 7, 1941, Paul Berger, another Lepke aide and former labor slugger, spent three hours on the witness stand depicting an underworld in which union officials and gangsters joined forces while witnesses were shot down in the street. He admitted being the "finger man" in a number of killings.

Berger explained how in 1936 he had fingered Joseph Rosen to Mendy Weiss several days before Rosen was murdered. He also admitted to pointing out his former friend, Max Rubin, to various gunmen on three different occasions. Berger went on to tell how he worked as a collector for Lepke in his garment-center rackets.

Questioned by Assistant D.A. Turkus, Berger said that two days before the Rosen slaying, he was told by Max Rubin that Lepke wanted to see him. He said he went to Lepke's sixth-floor offices on Fifth Avenue. Berger related that Lepke said to him, "I want you to point out Joe Rosen," whom Berger had known through business transactions. Lepke then took Berger in a taxi to the Lower East Side where they met Mendy Weiss. Weiss drove Berger to Brooklyn where Berger pointed out Rosen. According to Berger, Weiss got out of the car and passed by Rosen's store several times. "I'll know him now," Weiss said. Two days later, Berger said, he read about Rosen being shot and killed.[59]

On November 12, 1941, Abe "Kid Twist" Reles, the prosecution's star witness in the Murder Inc. cases, was thrown from his sixth-floor-room window in the Half Moon Hotel at Coney Island. Reles had been kept under police protection at the Half Moon for months. Five detectives worked around the clock at the hotel, supposedly guarding the Combination witnesses that were quartered there. A wire had been attached to a radiator in Reles's room to make it look like he had tried to escape and fell.[60] Although he was scheduled to appear as a witness against Lepke, his death had little impact on the Rosen murder case as the prosecution had already accumulated sufficient evidence.

According to Charles "Lucky" Luciano some twenty years later, "The truth of the whole thing was that the whole bunch of cops was on the take and Bals handled the whole thing." Frank Bals was the acting police captain who was in charge of the witness-protection detail. Luciano continued, "We paid him fifty grand and set aside some more money for the other guys in case they hadda take a rap. The way I heard it was that Bals stood there in the room and supervised the whole thing. Reles was sleepin' and one of the cops give him a tap with a billy and knocked him out. Then they picked him up and heaved him out the window. For Chrissake, he landed so far from the wall he couldn'tve done that even if he jumped."[61]

Up until this point in the trial, the combined stories of Lepke's lieutenants could not convict. Sholem Bernstein and Berger, as wheelman and finger, would have to be corroborated. Max Rubin was not an accomplice, but he could tell none of the assassination details beyond the moment that Lepke blew up and threatened to take care of Joe Rosen. Louis Capone had been linked as the production director of the Rosen contract only through Sholem Bernstein's unsubstantiated story. Mendy Weiss's role as triggerman as described by Bernstein was also uncorroborated.

The only thing the prosecution witnesses got across to the court was that Lepke was angry and he asked Berger to point out Joe Rosen to Mendy Weiss. Part of Lepke's criminal genius was his remarkable talent to cover himself. Lepke, like many other criminals, made one mistake, and he apparently never even realized it. This mistake materialized in court the day Albert "Allie" Tannenbaum, Lepke labor slugger and gunman, took the witness stand against his former boss. Allie had never entered the Rosen murder case until the moment he was called to testify. He was the only man in the world through whom the law could cash in on Lepke's lone mistake in the Joe Rosen murder.[62]

Albert "Allie" Tannenbaum became a state witness in April 1940. Faced with several murder indictments, Allie decided that it would be to his advantage to get on the bandwagon like his old associate, Abe Reles, had. Tannenbaum had been living at the Half Moon Hotel in the same suite of rooms as Abe Reles. Like Reles, he had been under the twenty-four-hour, around-the-clock protection of the D.A.'s office. On November 13, 1941, he took the witness stand for the prosecution in the Rosen murder trial. Pale and obviously shaken by the death of Reles, whose room was next to his, Tannenbaum began to testify against his underworld bosses.

Tannenbaum said that he had been on Lepke's payroll since 1931. He started as a $35-a-week labor slugger and strong-arm man and worked his way up to a $125-a-week gunman. According to Tannenbaum, he performed general assignments and murder jobs for Lepke. Tannenbaum admitted to the court that he had taken part in six murders and described his general assignments as killing, being a finger man, acting as a lookout in other crimes, and assisting in the disposal of victims' bodies.[63] He went on to describe how he participated in fifty sluggings and had thrown more than 100 stench bombs in labor disputes.[64]

Allie Tannenbaum took his orders from Gurrah and Mendy Weiss. According to Allie, "Lep told me to do what they say." Allie, however, made his assignment reports to Lepke personally at Lepke's private office at Raleigh Manufacturing Company on lower Fifth Avenue in Manhattan. In the late summer of 1936, Tannenbaum had killed Irv Ashkenaz, a taxi operator who was talking to Dewey assistant district attorneys about the cab racket in New York.

The Friday before Joe Rosen was murdered, Tannenbaum went up to Lepke's office to report. When he walked in, Lepke was with Max Rubin and in a rage. It was the first time Tannenbaum had ever seen the boss upset. According to Allie, "Lepke was yelling that he gave Joe Rosen money to go away and then he sneaks back into a candy store after he tells him to stay away. Lepke was hollering, he says, 'There is one son of a bitch that will never go to talk to Dewey about me.' Max [Rubin] was trying to calm him down. He was saying, 'Take it easy, take it easy, Louis, I'll handle Joe Rosen all right.'"

"What did Lepke say to that?" asked Prosecutor Turkus.

"He says, 'You told me that before.' He says, 'This is the end of it, I'm fed up with that son of a bitch.' He says, 'I'll take care of him.'"

Allie substantiated how Max Rubin begged Lepke to let Rubin get the trucking-union officials to straighten out Rosen. Allie had never seen Lepke blow up. Two nights later, he said, he read in the paper that Rosen was murdered, and the name clicked. The day after reading about the slaying, Monday, September 14, 1936, Tannenbaum dropped into Lepke's office. He was sitting there when Mendy Weiss walked in. (This was the day after the Rosen murder.)

"What was said?" asked the prosecutor.

"Lepke says was everything all right. Mendy says everything is okay only that SOB 'Pep' [Harry Strauss]. He says, 'I give him strict orders not to do any shooting, but after I shoot Rosen and he's laying on the floor, he starts shooting at him.' Lepke says, 'All right, what's the difference as long as everybody is clean and you got away all right,' and he pats Mendy on the back."

Assistant Prosecutor Burton Turkus remembered that "For perhaps half-a-dozen seconds, you could have heard a beetle blink in the courtroom." Allie Tannenbaum's testimony corroborated Max Rubin's story on Lepke, corroborated Sholem Bernstein's account of the murder and Mendy Weiss's role as one of the gunmen, and Tannenbaum was not even remotely involved or connected to the Rosen job himself. Allie Tannenbaum had all but unlocked the door to the death house for his longtime business associates.

Lepke almost never gave out a contract directly to gunmen in his mob. That is why he told Tannenbaum to take his orders from Mendy or Gurrah. Lepke had been so enraged that the little man in the little candy store would dare defy the mighty Lepke with all of his connections and all of his gunmen that afterward he did not even recall that Tannenbaum was sitting in the room at the time. If his rage hadn't blinded him into forgetfulness, Allie would have soon followed Joe Rosen. Allie's corroboration had the potential of putting Lepke and Weiss in the electric chair. Louis Capone's counsel, however, was unperturbed. So far about the only thing Capone could be charged with in 2,400 pages of testimony was that he did not associate with the right people.

Berger had related how Mendy Weiss had stopped for a moment to talk to Louis Capone on a Brownsville street corner the day that Berger fingered Joe Rosen. It could be inferred that Weiss had talked to Capone to have him begin preparing the Rosen murder contract, but guesses are not proof in a court of law. Sholem Bernstein's testimony of how Louis Capone had drilled him on the Rosen murder getaway route was not corroborated. In reality, though, Louis Capone had made the same mistake as Lepke, and he had forgotten all about it. He was having a quiet conversation in his home three-and-a-half years after the Rosen murder and had put his foot in his mouth. The prosecution had been saving Seymour "Blue Jaw" Magoon to show exactly how.[65]

On November 15, 1941, Magoon described his association with the Combination that he "shot two fellows who did not die," that he had driven automobiles used in two murders, and that he had stolen cars used in crimes for the murder ring.[66] Magoon was questioned by Assistant D.A. Turkus.

"In April 1939, did Capone speak to you in reference to a man named Friedman?"

"Yes," responded Magoon.

"Were you told to do something in reference to this man?"

"Yes."

Magoon was ordered to help Harry Strauss kill Whitey Friedman. Magoon looked over the area of the planned murder and did not like what he saw.

"Where did you go?" asked the prosecutor.

"I went to his [Capone's] house, we were in the parlor."

"What did you say?"

"I asked Capone if it was advisable for me to work on the Friedman thing because I hung out only a block away right off Sutter Avenue."

During the conversation, Capone had tossed out a remark putting him right in the center of the Rosen murder. In legal parlance, any declaration against interest by a defendant may be introduced against him no matter how he said it or to whom. It is allowed.

"Did Capone answer?"

"Capone says, 'What are you worried about?' I said, 'I am not worried, Louie. I'm just asking for advice,' and Capone says, 'I worked on the Rosen thing, and it was right on Sutter Avenue, and I wasn't recognized.'"

That single sentence, "I worked on the Rosen thing," had come back to haunt Capone. Magoon, who was personally involved in a number of crimes, but connected in no way with the murder of Joseph Rosen, provided the necessary corroboration for all Berger and Sholem Bernstein had said about Capone. In spite of this, courtroom experts believed that Capone had a good chance if he would take the witness stand in his own defense and gamble getting through cross-examination with a whole skin. But suddenly and dramatically, Capone's counsel rested without offering a word of defense, not even his own.[67]

On November 17, 1941, as the trial was entering its tenth week, the state rested its case. The prosecution presented its evidence through thirty-three witnesses and fifty-seven exhibits to establish its contention that Joseph Rosen was driven out of business and then slain at Lepke's direction because the racket boss feared that Rosen would testify against him before Special Prosecutor Thomas E. Dewey. A thirty-fourth witness would have been Abe "Kid Twist" Reles, who had mysteriously died the week before.[68]

For the defense, Lepke led the team. He did not take the stand himself, but brought in seven different witnesses to speak for him. The gist of the defense argument was why would a powerful racketeer be annoyed with a small-time trucker like Joe Rosen who basically knew nothing about Lepke's operation? The defense also argued that neither Max Rubin nor Allie Tannenbaum had been in Lepke's office on Friday, September 11, 1936, the day he reportedly blew up and vowed to get Rosen,.[69]

One of Lepke's witnesses was Nat Sobler, a partner of Joe Rosen's in the New York and New Jersey Trucking Company. As a witness for the defense, Sobler was supposed to testify that the New York and New Jersey Trucking Company had never been a good business and that the employees were often paid with bad checks. On two different occasions, Sobler lost his temper and tried to leave the courtroom.[70] Each time he was stopped by a bailiff. Sobler's testimony held little weight once the prosecution disclosed that they had a signed affidavit from Sobler who a month earlier had told the D.A.'s office that "there was a good living" for Rosen and their trucking partners from their firm. Sobler added at the time he signed the affidavit, that after the work stoppage of 1932 (conceived by Lepke), the company's key accounts were taken away and went to Garfield Express, the company in which Lepke became a partner.

Carl Shapiro, Gurrah's brother, appeared as a witness for Lepke. He was treasurer of the Raleigh Manufacturing Company where Lepke had his private office. Shapiro claimed neither Tannenbaum nor Rubin was in Lepke's office on September 11, 1936, because he had been there all day signing checks. The prosecution destroyed this argument by showing there was nothing to stop Shapiro from having New York checks (which were a different color) mailed from the Baltimore offices of the firm to New York or signing postdated or blank checks on any day. Carl Shapiro went on to say that "Mr. Buchalter does not yell. I don't believe I ever heard Mr. Buchalter raise his voice. He had very little to say at all times."[71]

Jacob "Gurrah" Shapiro was even brought to New York from federal prison. If he testified, he was expected to deny that he had ever gone over Rosen's books and told him what firms he could not do business with. He was never called by the defense.[72]

Last but not least was the Mendy Weiss defense.

Mendy's attorneys argued that on the night of September 12, 1936, Mendy could not have possibly been in the vicinity of Joe Rosen's Brooklyn candy store casing the neighborhood because he had thrown a birthday party for his younger brother, Sidney, who was to turn twenty-six on the thirteenth. This was on the urging of his mother to patch up a family quarrel. The two brothers, their mother, Mendy's wife, and a girlfriend had supposedly driven uptown, had dinner, attended a show, and then had a snack before returning home at 4:00 A.M.[73]

Sidney Weiss was asked by the prosecution, "Of all the birthdays in your life, this twenty-sixth birthday was the only one you celebrated?"

"That is right," said Sidney Weiss.

Other information about Sidney Weiss visiting his brother in Kansas City when he was on the lam was presented by the prosecution in cross-examination. Louis Capone did not take the stand and did not have any alibi witness. The defense attorneys took three days for their summation. The keynote of the defense summation was that Lepke and his two associates were the victims of an immense frame-up. Lepke's attorneys denounced Tannenbaum and Magoon as pampered thugs who were all a part of a frame-up scheme engineered by Max Rubin, who blamed Lepke for shooting him in the head in 1937. Their arguments were weak.[74]

At 1:15 P.M. on Saturday, November 29, 1941, the fates of Lepke, his lieutenant, and his gunman were placed in the hands of the jury. Announcement of a verdict was declared at 2:45 A.M. November 30, 1941. The jury had been out four-and-a-half hours.[75] Jury foreman Charles E. Stevens rose and opened the envelope. "We find the defendants, and each of them, guilty of murder in the first degree as charged." Lepke showed no emotion, but slowly wiped a bead of perspiration from his forehead with a handkerchief. On December 2, 1941, the three defendants were all sentenced to death the first week of January 1942 in the Sing Sing electric chair.[76]

For Mendy Weiss and Louis Capone, there were no legal impediments to prevent their execution the first week of January 1942. For Lepke, there was still a great deal of legal confusion about his pending federal-prisoner status. It would still be more than two years before the three thugs would meet their fate.

12 The Last Days of Lepke

"Louis Buchalter alias Lepke for the murder of Joseph Rosen whereof he is convicted is hereby sentenced to the punishment of death. Within ten days from this date subject to any legal impediments the Sheriff of Kings County shall deliver the said Louis Buchalter to the warden of Sing Sing Prison where he shall be kept in solitary confinement until the week beginning with Sunday January 4, 1942 and upon some day within that week so appointed, the warden of Sing Sing Prison shall do execution upon him, the said Louis Buchalter alias Lepke in the mode and manner prescribed by law."[1]

—Judge Franklin Taylor
December 2, 1941

Judge Taylor repeated the same death-sentence proclamation to Louis Capone and Emanuel "Mendy" Weiss. News of Lepke and his codefendants' conviction in the Rosen murder case was enlightening. It was the first time that the death sentence had been imposed on a gang leader and a man reputed by law-enforcement authorities to be a ranking member of the national Combination of organized crime. Lepke was the first of the three defendants to be sentenced. White-faced and obviously under a great deal of emotional strain, Lepke walked into the courtroom with his lawyers. Working his tongue inside his cheek, he grasped the railing of the clerk's bench with both hands and braced himself for the sentencing pronouncement.

189

Weiss was sentenced next. The hulking and powerful-ly built man was red with anger as his death sentence was pronounced. When asked if he had anything to say, he blurted hotly, "All I can say is I'm innocent."

Louis Capone was the last to be sentenced and the calmest of the three, although it was feared that he might collapse because of a serious heart condition.

U.S. Attorney Harold Kennedy moved to have Mendy Weiss's $115,000 bail bond canceled in his federal drug indictment so that he could be turned over to the state of New York. Leaving the courtroom, Weiss turned to Assistant Prosecutor Burton Turkus and said, "You got my blood. How that Captain Bals can frame a guy." Bals was in charge of the Brooklyn D.A.'s detective squad. Weiss's comment was provoked when Bals told him, "Peter Panto is waiting for you."[2] Panto was a longshoreman union leader that Weiss strangled to death in 1939 as a favor to Albert Anastasia.

Within forty-eight hours, Weiss and Capone were shuttled off to the Sing Sing death house to await execu-tion. Lepke remained in federal custody at the govern-ment detention center in Manhattan.[3] He would remain there while the murder conviction of Lepke and his code-fendants was appealed. D.A. William O'Dwyer believed that if the guilty verdict was sustained, it might be neces-sary for the president to either pardon or commute Lepke's narcotics-smuggling sentence in order to allow the government to legally turn him over to the state of New York. A Justice Department spokesman told the press that customarily, a federal prisoner had to serve his sentence before he could be turned over to the state for imprisonment or execution. D.A. O'Dwyer explained that under the terms of the federal court order, Lepke was to be returned to federal custody following sentencing by the state.[4]

The Brooklyn D.A.'s office thought that there was legal precedent that would help in getting Lepke transferred to state jurisdiction. The precedent was established in the case of Gerald Chapman. Chapman was a bank robber and the nation's first Public Enemy Number 1. In October 1921, he and two accomplices staged the Leonard Street mail robbery in Manhattan, taking more than a million dollars in cash and securities. (This was the largest robbery in U.S. history up until that time.)[5] Chapman was eventually caught and sentenced to twenty-five years in federal prison. He escaped twice from Atlanta. On his second escape, as a fugitive, he robbed a New Britain, Connecticut, department store and killed a police officer. He was apprehended and tried by the state, where he was convicted of first-degree murder and sentenced to hang.

His attorneys argued that he must first serve his federal sentence. Chapman was given a presidential commutation of sentence, which opened the way for his execution by the state. Chapman, through his attorney, appealed to the U.S. Supreme Court for a review of the case and challenged the right of the president to commute the sentence of a federal prisoner against his will. It was Chapman's counsel's contention that he never accepted the presidential commutation, and therefore, it was not valid.

The Supreme Court reviewed the case and handed down a decision finding that the presidential commutation was legal and valid. It was not necessary for the subject of a sentence to accept or refuse a commutation. A commutation of sentence was in itself a legal act that allowed for no discretion on the part of the person concerned.[6] The Supreme Court ruled that a pardon was a gift and therefore could be refused. A commutation was not a gift, but the withdrawal of restraining powers and claims. William Howard Taft, as chief justice of the U.S. Supreme Court, held, "The penitentiary is no sanctuary and may not be used as immunity from capital law." In 1927, Chapman was hung for the murder in Connecticut.[7]

This was the beginning of a lengthy legal battle over custody of Lepke that would continue for more than two years. The question of whether President Franklin Delano Roosevelt would pardon or commute Lepke's federal sentence would not be answered until all of the mobster's legal appeals were exhausted.[8] Lepke was the first gang leader ever convicted of first-degree murder for a killing performed by a subordinate.[9] Now his attorneys would use every legal ploy to prevent Lepke from being turned over to the state of New York. A member of Lepke's defense team told the press that they would apply for a writ of habeas corpus if necessary to block his removal from federal custody to the New York State death house in Ossining.[10]

Less than one hour after the three men were convicted, Lepke's counsel talked about appealing directly to the U.S. Supreme Court on the startling contention that Lepke was deprived of his constitutional rights when he was tried and convicted by New York State while still a federal prisoner.[11]

The following is a chronological account of Lepke's legal process from when the State Court of Appeals upheld his and his codefendants' murder convictions on October 30, 1942.

October 30, 1942—State Court of Appeals upheld the conviction of the three men. The court fixed the week of December 7, 1942, as the week within which the death sentences would be carried out. It was explained that in the final stage, the question of whether Lepke would be executed under the state murder conviction or would be confined to federal prison for the duration of his fourteen-year term would rest with President Roosevelt. Under this procedure, application is made for the commutation of the federal sentence, and then the U.S. attorney general submits a request for commutation stating his opinion on the matter to the president for his approval or disapproval. The Brooklyn D.A. would request a conditional pardon, the condition being that if Lepke received clemency from the governor and the death sentence would be commuted to life in prison, he would have to be returned to the feds to finish his fourteen-year sentence first.[12]

November 9, 1942—The Brooklyn D.A.'s office wrote a letter to the Pardon Division of the Department of Justice. On December 6, 1942, the three men received a stay of execution from December 10, 1942, until January 4, 1943, to permit defense attorneys to appeal the decision of the New York Court of Appeals to the U.S. Supreme Court.[13] On January 3, 1943, another order granting a stay of execution was served on John A. Lyons, New York State corrections commissioner, from U.S. Supreme Court Justice Owen J. Roberts on the condition that a writ of certiorari be filed by defense attorneys. The stay of execution was extended until the Supreme Court ruled on the case.[14] At first, on February 16, 1943, the Supreme Court decided not to review the case. Then, on

March 16, 1943, the Court agreed to review the convictions of Lepke, Weiss, and Capone after counsel for the three men presented the Court with another brief.[15]

June 1, 1943—The U.S. Supreme Court, by unanimous decision, again upheld the convictions of Lepke and his two aides. The second appeal to the Court was based on what Lepke said was the poisoned atmosphere at the time of the trial. The four-page opinion handed down by the Court rejected the three convicted murderers' claim that they did not have an impartial jury, that Judge Taylor was biased, and that the Brooklyn D.A. resorted to unfair tactics to influence the jurors.[16]

July 8, 1943—The Brooklyn D.A.'s office appealed to U.S. Attorney General Francis Biddle for the release of Lepke to the state of New York. Acting Brooklyn District Attorney Thomas Craddock Hughes asked Biddle to free Lepke so that he could be turned over to New York State for execution. By this time, both Weiss and Capone, as individuals, had unsuccessfully sought reversals of their first-degree murder convictions from the New York State Court of Appeals and the U.S. Supreme Court. In order to get Lepke to the Sing Sing death house, his federal sentence would still have to be commuted by President Roosevelt. Daniel M. Lyons, a pardon attorney with the U.S. Department of Justice, informed Mr. Hughes that his office was not persuaded to recommend that the attorney general take steps to terminate the federal imprisonment of Lepke. The state of New York did not intend to execute Weiss and Capone until Lepke was turned over by federal authorities.

Again, in his letter to the Department of Justice, Acting D.A. Hughes quoted Supreme Court Chief Justice Taft's opinion in the case of *Kelley v. Oregon.* "A prisoner may certainly be tried, convicted and sentenced for another crime committed prior to or during his imprisonment and may suffer capital punishment and be executed during the term. The penitentiary is no sanctuary and life in it does not confer immunity from capital punishment provided by law. He has no vested constitutional right to serve out his unexpired sentence!"

Hughes wrote, "Under the circumstances I therefore hereby make formal application to you personally as Attorney General of the U.S. for your recommendation to the president for the commutation of Buchalter in order that the death penalty may be executed upon him by the State of New York pursuant to sentence."[17]

July 10, 1943—Justice Department officials refused to advise Lepke's release for resentencing and execution. Because the time had elapsed since the three men were to be executed originally, New York State law required that sentence be reimposed on them. The New York State law also required that the sentence be made by the New York Court of Appeals rather than the trial judge.[18]

July 17, 1943—The Justice Department informed the judges of the New York State Court of Appeals that Lepke and his codefendants would be made available for resentencing.[19]

July 20, 1943—Lepke, Mendy, and Capone were resentenced to death for the week of September 13, 1943, by the New York State Court of Appeals. The execution of Lepke was still dependent upon presidential action. Weiss and Capone's attorneys planned an appeal to Governor Dewey for commutation of their death sentences to life imprisonment on the grounds that they had an unfair trial.

Governor Dewey would appeal to President Roosevelt to release Lepke to the state for a decision as to whether he would die or be sentenced to life imprisonment. The execution date was set for September 16, 1943.[20]

September 2, 1943—Gov. Thomas Dewey demanded that President Roosevelt pardon Lepke to permit his execution. A new execution date was set for October 18, 1943. Pending the surrender of Lepke to the state of New York, the governor deferred the executions of Emanuel "Mendy" Weiss and Louis Capone. The governor stated that it would be unfair to give Lepke a haven in federal prison while his two henchmen were sent to the chair. Governor Dewey made the following statement. "I shall refuse to set a date for a clemency hearing for the two lesser figures until Buchalter is surrendered by the President to be dealt with in accordance with law. Respites have been executed by me today deferring the executions in these cases from the week beginning September 13, 1943 to the week beginning October 18, 1943, awaiting the necessary surrender of Buchalter to the State by the President."[21]

October 7, 1943—The Brooklyn D.A.'s office again appealed to Attorney General Biddle (no answer was received for the request issued July 8).

October 14, 1943—A new execution date was set for November 29. Governor Dewey cited President Roosevelt's failure to release Lepke. Again Dewey declared that he would not order the executions of Weiss and Capone while the boss remained alive.[22]

October 18, 1943—The federal D.A. for New York suggested to the Brooklyn D.A. that Governor Dewey hold a clemency hearing. If the governor refused clemency, the feds would turn over Lepke to the state. The state of New York attorney general pointed out that a clemency hearing is incongruous without the custody of the prisoner. Besides, no announcement is ever made when clemency is refused. The governor would remain silent, and the execution would take place.

October 20, 1943—The U.S. attorney general's office in a letter to the Brooklyn D.A. referred to "the understanding." The D.A. pointed out that there had been no understanding and that the New York federal attorney merely made a suggestion.

November 20, 1943—Governor Dewey charged that Lepke "was protected from punishment by the failure of the President of the United States to grant the customary conditional pardon." Dewey set the execution date back once again to January 3, 1944. Governor Dewey explained that unless the president gave Lepke a pardon, he could not be turned over to the state for execution. Past practice was that the president in such circumstances granted a conditional pardon or a commutation of sentence to such a prisoner. The governor could then hold an executive clemency hearing. If the prisoner received clemency, the conditional pardon granted by the president would become inoperative, and the prisoner would then be returned to the feds to complete his federal sentence. In a statement to the press, Dewey explained, "I have twice respited the executions of Capone and Weiss while the principal defendant is protected from punishment by the failure of the President of the United States to grant the customary conditional pardon."

Three specific requests for a conditional pardon or commutation of sentence had been made to the U.S. Justice Department. A Justice Department spokesman told the press:

The Attorney General has made it plain in correspondence with the Acting D.A. [of Brooklyn] at such time as the governor of New York has ruled on Buchalter's clemency petition and advises the Attorney General that the State is ready to carry out sentence imposed by the State Court prompt consideration will be given to commutation of the Federal sentence. The Attorney General will not recommend the release of Buchalter from his Federal sentence as long as any possibility exists that his State sentence might also be commuted.[23]

November 30, 1943—U.S. Attorney General Biddle refused to make a formal request of the president for the commutation of Lepke's sentence (second anniversary of Lepke's conviction). At this point, Biddle criticized Governor Dewey for choosing to communicate through the newspapers with the president. He again stated that if New York would hold a clemency hearing, the government would produce Lepke. Then, if Buchalter's sentence was in any way modified by the state, he would have to serve his federal time.[24] New York State Attorney General Nathan L. Goldstein then wrote the U.S. Attorney General that Governor Dewey would not assure federal authorities that Lepke would be executed if he was granted a conditional pardon by President Roosevelt. He added that the governor could not grant a clemency hearing until Lepke was in state custody. Mr. Goldstein stated, "I fail to understand the curious reluctance to treat this case in the usual manner."[25]

Dark rumors began to circulate that perhaps the Roosevelt administration hesitated to turn Lepke over to New York because he knew too much about certain political figures. There might also be the possibility that

198

Governor Dewey would cut a deal with Lepke if he agreed to talk about his past connections to certain New Deal labor leaders with whom he had dealings or had once done business. This would be a perfect way for the politically ambitious Dewey, who had presidential aspirations, to discredit the popular Roosevelt administration and the Democratic Party.[26] At this point, Governor Dewey postponed the execution of the three men for the fourth time to February 6, 1944. (Dewey had postponed the executions on September 1, October 15, and November 29, 1943.)[27]

In an article dated January 3, 1944, *Newsweek* claimed that by the last week in December of 1943, there were strong indications that the feds were finally going to turn Lepke over to New York State. According to this article, this latest move by the federal government in the six-month-old dispute came too late to head off strong suspicions of politicking and political maneuverings on the part of the Roosevelt administration in preparation for the 1944 presidential battle.

Scripps-Howard columnist Westbrook Pegler brought the issue into the open. According to Pegler, "(1) During his racketeering days, Lepke controlled Local 4 of the Cutters Union of the Amalgamated Clothing Workers of America. (2) Amalgamated's head was and still is Sidney Hillman, New Deal favorite and once co-director of the nation's defense program. (3) Governor Dewey, who as New York County D.A., knew this and suspected that Lepke could tell plenty about New Dealers' relations with racketeers. (4) Therefore, Dewey would not promise to execute Lepke without giving him a clemency hearing and the offer of mercy if he should talk." Pegler's conclusion: President Roosevelt was refusing to hand over Lepke to New York in order to protect Hillman.[28] None of this argument could be proven, yet it still provided the public with food for thought.

January 17, 1944—Attorney General Biddle offered a compromise. The state of New York would be given full authority over Lepke for a clemency hearing. If clemency was refused, the president would then pardon Lepke so he could be executed by the state. According to the newspapers, the government offered Dewey this concession because the case was becoming too hot for the Roosevelt administration to handle during an election year. At this point, the execution date was set for the week beginning February 7, 1944. It was again suggested by the press that the Roosevelt administration feared turning Lepke over to the state because it was afraid that in order to cut a deal to save himself from the chair, he would make public statements about his past labor racketeering that would involve persons close to the administration.[29]

On January 21, 1944, Lepke was officially turned over to the state of New York on a conditional pardon, the condition being that if his sentence was commuted to life by the governor, he must be returned to the feds to finish out the remaining ten years of his drug sentence. That same day, Lepke was taken to the Sing Sing death house from the Federal Detention Center in Manhattan. After being fingerprinted and photographed at Sing Sing, Lepke was asked the customary question by the receiving officer. "To what do you attribute your criminal act?" "Not guilty," replied Lepke.[30] Weiss and Capone had been in the Sing Sing death house since December 1941.

On January 21, 1944, Mendy Weiss's attorneys filed a motion for a new trial. This was based on affidavits from

Louis Maione and his sister, Jennie Daddona. They assert-ed that when they visited Harry "Happy" Maione (Combination hit man sentenced to death in 1941 at Sing Sing), he told them Weiss and Capone could not have committed the Rosen murder because he had. Another condemned Murder Inc. hit man, Irving Nitzberg, claimed he heard Maione make this statement. Harry Maione and Frank Abbundando were executed in January 1942.[31] Once Lepke arrived at the Sing Sing death house, he was not allowed to see or speak to his fellow defen-dants. The three men were scheduled to be executed February 10, 1944. On January 28, 1944, Judge Franklin Taylor of Kings County denied the motion for a new trial based on the Maione affidavits.[32]

On February 3, 1944, Governor Dewey finally held the clemency hearing for the three men. Their attorneys requested that a special commission be appointed to investigate the facts of their murder trial. It is interesting that this request was made after the U.S. Supreme Court had upheld the convictions on two different occasions.[33] As their time ran out, the three men grasped at anything that might delay their execution. The defendants' attor-neys stated at the clemency hearing that D.A. O'Dwyer, then a lieutenant colonel in the army, was prepared to rec-ommend executive clemency for Lepke, Weiss, and Capone. A phone call by Acting Brooklyn D.A. Hughes quickly dispelled this after talking to O'Dwyer.[34] On February 27, 1944, the state executioner, Joseph Francel, was told to report to the Sing Sing death house to carry out the executions of Lepke, Weiss, and Capone on March 2, 1944.[35]

Lepke's attorney, who was still trying desperately to

stay his execution again, filed a writ of habeas corpus maintaining that the gang boss's transfer from federal-government custody to the state of New York was illegal.[36] Federal District Court refused the writ on March 2, 1944. The U.S. Circuit Court of Appeals affirmed the refusal.

It was now March 2, 1944, execution day. The condemned killers were shaved, bathed, and dressed in the conventional white socks, carpet slippers, and black trousers that were slit up one leg to allow the electrode to be laid upon bare skin. Customarily, condemned men are allowed to have last-day meals of their choice. Lepke ordered steak, French-fried potatoes, salad, and pie for lunch, and roast chicken, shoestring potatoes, salad, and pie for dinner. Weiss and Capone followed the boss and opted for the same.

At 9:40 P.M. (an hour and twenty minutes before the three men would walk their last mile), the governor granted a forty-eight-hour stay of execution because the U.S. Supreme Court had granted a last-ditch review of the habeas-corpus proceeding.[37] Late in the afternoon of March 2, 1944, Manhattan D.A. Frank Hogan received a message from the Sing Sing warden that Lepke wanted to talk to him. The fact that the three men were convicted in Brooklyn and Hogan was from Manhattan was not lost on the newspapers.

Hogan spoke to Lepke for an hour and a half in his cell. Later, word of the two-day stay was received. Hogan had returned to the city and telephoned Dewey. Whatever Lepke told Hogan was never made public. The governor's office insisted that the delay had nothing to do with the conversation and was only granted for the Supreme Court to review the habeas-corpus writ.

During the two-day stay of execution, the newspapers ran wild with speculation as to what Lepke revealed. Chief among the rumors was that Lepke could provide information against Sidney Hillman, president of the Amalgamated Clothing Workers of America and a member of President Roosevelt's wartime administration. It was believed that Dewey could link Lepke to Hillman and create a corruption scandal surrounding the Democrats that could hang over the party in the November 1944 elections.[38]

Preparations for the execution continued as the convicted trio waited for word from the attorneys on the Supreme Court's decision. The execution was scheduled for 11:00 P.M., Saturday, March 4, 1944. It would be the first Saturday on which an execution was scheduled in the Sing Sing death house since 1917.

On March 3, Governor Dewey indicated that he would not grant the three men another stay of execution.

Warden William E. Snyder of Sing Sing Prison told the press that the three condemned men's spiritual needs would be taken care of the night of the execution by Rabbi Jacob Katz, the Jewish chaplain at the prison.

Early on the morning of Friday, March 3, 1944, Rabbi Katz phoned the governor and asked that the executions not be held on Saturday, the day of the Jewish Sabbath. Rabbi Katz, who was the rabbi of Pelham Parkway Jewish Center in the Bronx, explained his request saying that he felt he needed more time to prepare Lepke and his henchmen for their fate. Because of Sabbath services, Rabbi Katz stated that he could not leave for the prison until sundown, and that would only give him about three hours with Lepke and with Weiss.

"It has been the custom for the chaplain to be with the condemned the whole day long on the last day of his life," Katz said. "It creates a very human feeling between the condemned and the chaplain and society and with his God, so much so that whatever nervousness, whatever tension has been created is reduced to a state of resignation and submission to one's fate on the part of the condemned." Katz made it plain that if the governor saw fit not to change the time of execution, he would have a car waiting after evening services to take him to the prison where he should arrive shortly after 8:00 P.M.[39]

On Saturday, March 4, 1944, the U.S. Supreme Court denied the final appeal without comment. Shortly afterward, Lepke's last statement was read by his wife at a meeting called at the Depot Square Hotel in Ossining, New York.[40]

"I am anxious to have it clearly understood that I did not offer to talk and give information in exchange for any promise of commutation of my death sentence. I did not ask for that. I insist that I am not guilty of the Rosen murder, that the witnesses against me lied, and that I did not receive a fair trial. Four out of seven judges of the Court of Appeals said that Weiss, Capone and I were not guilty. Judge Rippey [Harlan W. Rippey of the Court of Appeals] said we were not given even a remote outside chance of any fair consideration of our defense by the jury and that the evidence wasn't even enough to submit to the jury.

"The one and only thing I have asked for is to have a commission appointed to examine the facts in the Rosen case. If that examination does not show I am not guilty, I am willing to go to the chair regardless of what information I have given or can give."[41]

Buchalter was inaccurate in his statement that four Court of Appeals judges out of seven believed he and his two codefendants got an unfair trial, as the conviction of all three was upheld. Actually, four judges upheld the trial verdict and three dissented.[42]

According to the Assistant Brooklyn D.A., Burton B. Turkus, "By releasing the statement through his wife, Lepke also was, I am convinced, giving an unmistakable signal to the mob. He was broadcasting to his syndicate associates that he had not and would not talk of them or of the national cartel. About politicians and political connection and the like—yes; the crime magnates would seek no reprisal for that. But not about the top bosses of crime. It was pure and simple life insurance. No member of his family would be safe if the crime chiefs believed he had opened up on the organization itself."[43]

It was Saturday night, March 4, 1944. The condemned men once again ate their last supper and were prepared for execution. A telephone line from the governor's mansion in Albany was held open to the Sing Sing warden's office. At 10:55 P.M., the warden made a last check to see if the governor's office had called. There was no change. Society was finally through with Lepke Buchalter.

It was decided that Capone would be executed first because of his heart condition. At 11:02, Capone entered the Sing Sing death chamber flanked by two guards and the Rev. Bernard M. Martin, Roman Catholic chaplain of the prison. Thirty-six people were to witness the executions, mostly members of the press and various state officials.

Capone plodded limply down the short corridor. Capone's graying hair, close shaven at the back of his head, bristled over his temples. His body quivered as he entered the execution chamber. He looked uncomprehending. He slowly surveyed the room. His small, chunky body sagged slightly as he was led the last few paces to the chair. He sat down in the chair resigned to his fate. The guards strapped him in, and three minutes later, he was pronounced dead by Charles C. Sweet, the Sing Sing physician.

Next, Emanuel "Mendy" Weiss entered the execution chamber. The large and now-flabby Weiss was flanked by two guards. Immediately in front of him walked Rabbi Katz, intoning prayers in Hebrew. Weiss took one step toward the chair, hesitated, and then opened his tightly compressed lips. "Can I say something?" he asked meekly. The warden nodded. Weiss continued. "I'm here on a framed-up case."

For a moment, he chewed on a wad of gum, then he continued. "And Governor Dewey knows it. I want to thank Judge Lehman, he knows me because I'm a Jew." Weiss stopped talking and sat down in the chair. His restraints were adjusted. "Give my love to my family and everything." These were his last words. At 11:10 P.M., Weiss was declared dead and wheeled out.

The door to the death chamber was slowly swung open, and Rabbi Katz stepped into the room. Two expressionless guards walked in, and between them was Lepke. His mouth opened a fraction of an inch, and his lower lip quivered. He gazed around the room at the witnesses on the benches.[44] The doelike softness was gone from Lepke's eyes as he entered the death chamber. His step was brisk, almost defiant, like a man with something unpleasant that has to be done.

Throughout the whole ordeal, Lepke remained calm.

He walked across the chamber and almost threw himself into the electric chair. He said nothing. The attendants tightened the restraining straps and made sure the one electrode was attached to his leg. As the head electrode was lowered into place, Lepke glanced up. That was the last thing he saw.

The warden signaled, and the switch was thrown. Twenty-two-hundred volts slammed into Lepke's body, the impact hurling his 165 pounds against the straps. The attendants bared Lepke's chest, and the physician applied the stethoscope. "I pronounce this man legally dead," he intoned. The body was loaded onto the stretcher and rolled into the autopsy room. Ironically, for all his power and killings, it was the murder of one little man that caught up with Lepke and ended him.[45]

On March 5, 1944, Louis "Lepke" Buchalter and Emanuel "Mendy" Weiss found a common resting ground. They were buried within a half hour of each other at Mount Hebron Cemetery in Flushing, Queens. Only family and close friends were in attendance. During the day, New York City Mayor LaGuardia was asked at City Hall to comment on the Lepke execution.

"Well, they certainly tried everything," LaGuardia said, referring to the many reprieves granted to Lepke.

"Will there be another Lepke in New York?" a reporter asked. The mayor replied, "Yes, there will be if we turn government over to the politicians. Take the rackets, the slot machines, gambling, that's where the Lepkes find their pickings and their prerequisites."[46]

The funeral of Louis Capone was held in Coney Island. It was a funeral in the Prohibition-era gangland tradition. There were five open cars carrying gaudy floral tributes and a forty-nine-automobile procession. Capone was buried at Holy Cross Cemetery, Brooklyn.[47]

Allie Tannenbaum and Seymour Magoon, the Murder Inc. gunmen that provided the necessary corroboration that put Lepke and his two aides in the chair, were later released in return for their testimony. In the early fifties, Tannenbaum was discovered in Atlanta, Georgia. The reformed gangster was now a lampshade salesman with a family. Albert Anastasia, the Mangano crime family underboss and overseer of Murder Inc., was never brought to justice.

After Buchalter's death in 1944, the garment-industry rackets were divided up among the five New York City crime families, which to some extent still control aspects of the business today.[48]

World War II brought prosperity to the garment industry, and racketeers were able to make their way in quiet comfort. This was mostly accomplished by keeping the needle-trade unions out of various shops. For this service, the New York underworld was paid handsomely. During the war, there was enough work for everyone. Former Lepke aides and partners emerged from World War II as garment-district entrepreneurs and union leaders.[49]

Lepke's Murder Inc. straw boss and close friend, Albert Anastasia, owned apparel factories and garment-center trucking companies. Harry Strasser, a Lepke aide, owned a garment-trucking company with fifty-five vans. Mafioso James Plumeri became a clothing manufacturer. Plumeri and his nephew, John "Johnny Dio" Dioguardi, were once sluggers for Lepke. Johnny Dio became a notorious labor racketeer in the fifties and sixties. Former Lepke strong-arm thug "Scarface" Louis Lieberman was receiving payoffs from almost 100 nonunion shops. The list went on and on.

In the late forties, former Lepke aide Sam Berger was president of garment-trucking Local 102 of the ILGWU. ILGWU President David Dubinsky was quoted as saying, "There's no point in kicking Berger out since his successor would probably be carried out feet first."

Just as in the old days, fear of underworld retaliation kept everyone quiet in the post-World War II garment industry. On May 9, 1949, ILGWU organizer William Lurye was stabbed to death in a West Thirty-fifth Street phone booth. He had made the fatal mistake of being one of a raiding party that invaded a loft and slashed a quantity of dresses belonging to a nonunion firm in which Albert Anastasia had an interest.[50] Anastasia deposed the Mangano brothers in 1950 and became boss of the Mangano crime family. In 1957, the lord high executioner of Murder Inc. was shot to death in a Manhattan barbershop. This was part of a coup staged by the ambitious Vito Genovese. Anastasia's underboss, Carlo Gambino, became head of the criminal organization that still bears his name.

The late fifties brought the first serious government investigations of racketeering in labor and management by the McClellan Committee. Hard evidence was finally surfacing as to the extent of the underworld's penetration of labor and unions.[51]

It was not until the late seventies and early eighties of the twentieth century that the federal government was able to effectively prosecute whole criminal organizations that had been involved in labor racketeering for decades. Through the use of the 1970 RICO Act, criminal syndicates that were manipulating garment manufacturers began to be destroyed once and for all. The legacy of Louis "Lepke" Buchalter and earlier labor sluggers continued long after these infamous labor racketeers disappeared from the scene.

Bibliography

Books

Abadinski, Howard. *Organized Crime.* Chicago: Nelson Hall, 1994.

Adamic, Louis. *Dynamite: The Story of Class Violence in America.* New York: Viking, 1931.

Alcorn, Robert Hayden. *The County of Gramercy Park: The Story of Gerald Chapman Gangster.* London: Hurst and Blackett, 1955.

Anslinger, Harry J., with Gursler, Will. *The Murderers: The Shocking Story of the Narcotics Gangs.* New York: Farrar, Straus and Cudahy, 1961.

Arm, Walter. *Pay-off: The Inside Story of Big City Corruption.* New York: Appleton-Century-Crofts, 1951.

Asbury, Herbert. *The Gangs of New York: An Informal History of the Underworld.* New York: Alfred Knopf, 1927.

Block, Alan. *Eastside-Westside: Organizing Crime in New York 1930-1950.* Cardiff, UK: University of Cardiff Press, 1980.

Clarke, Donald Henderson. *In the Reign of Rothstein.* New York: Vanguard Press, 1929.

Cohen, Rich. *Tough Jews: Fathers, Sons and Gangster Dreams.* New York: Simon and Schuster, 1998.

Cressey, Donald R. *Theft of the Nation: The Structure and Operations of*

Organized Crime in America. New York: Harper & Row, 1969.

Cummings, John and Ernest Volkman. *Goombata: The Improbable Rise and Fall of John Gotti and His Gang.* Boston: Little Brown, 1990.

Davis, John H. *Mafia Dynasty: The Rise and Fall of the Gambino Crime Family.* New York: Harper, Collins, 1993.

Dewey, Thomas E. *Twenty Against the Underworld.* Garden City, N.Y.: Doubleday, 1974.

Downey, Patrick. *Gangster City: The History of the New York Underworld 1900-1935.* New Jersey: Barricade Books, 2004.

Fox, Stephen. *Blood and Power: Organized Crime in Twentieth Century America.* New York: William Morrow, 1989.

Fried, Albert. *The Rise and Fall of the Jewish Gangster in America.* New York: Holt, Rhinehart and Winston, 1980.

Garrett, Charles. *The LaGuardia Years.* New Brunswick, N.J.: Rutgers University Press, 1961.

Goldin, Hyman E., ed. *Dictionary of American Underworld Lingo.* New York: Twayne Publishers, 1950.

Gosch, Martin A. and Richard Hammer. *The Last Testament of Lucky Luciano.* Boston: Little, Brown, 1975.

Hammer, Richard. *Playboy's Illustrated History of Organized Crime.* Chicago: Playboy Press, 1975.

Hearn, Daniel Allen. *Legal Executions in New York State 1639-1963.* Jefferson, N.C.: McFarland & Co, 1997.

Helmer, William with Rick Mattix. *Public Enemies: America's Criminal Past 1919-1940.* New York: Checkmark Books, 1998.

Hillquit, Morris. *Loose Leaves from a Busy Life.* New York: Macmillan Co, 1934.

Hughes, Rupert. *Attorney for the People: The Story of Thomas E. Dewey.* Boston: Houghton Mifflin, 1940.

Hutchinson, John. *The Imperfect Union: A History of Corruption in American Trade Unions.* New York: E.P. Dutton, 1970.

Irey, Elmer L. as told to William J. Slocum. *The Tax Dodgers: The Inside Story of the T-Men's War with America's Political and Underworld Hoodlums.* New York: Greenberg Publishing Co., 1948.

Jackson, Kenneth T. and John B. Manbock. *The Neighborhoods of Brooklyn.* New Haven and London: Yale University Press, 1998.

Jeffers, H. Paul. *Gentleman Gerald.* New York: St. Martin's Press, 1995.

Jennings, Dean. *We Only Kill Each Other: The Life and Bad Times of Bugsy Siegel.* Englewood Cliffs, N.J.: Prentice Hall, 1968.

Johnson, Malcom. *Crime on the Labor Front.* New York: Putnam, 1950.

Joselit, Jenna Weissman. *Our Gang: Jewish Crime and the New York Jewish Community, 1900-1940.* Bloomington: Indiana University Press, 1983.

Katcher, Leo. *The Big Bankroll: The Life and Times of Arnold Rothstein.* New York: Harper, 1959.

Kelly, J. Robert. *Encyclopedia of Organized Crime in the United States: From Capone's Chicago to the New Urban Underworld.* Westport, Conn.: Greenwood Press, 2000.

Lacey, Robert. *Little Man: Meyer Lansky and the Gangster Life.* Boston: Little, Brown, 1991.

Levine, Gary. *Anatomy of a Gangster: Jack "Legs" Diamond.* Cranbury, N.J.: A. S. Barnes, 1979.

Logan, Andy. *Against the Evidence: The Becker Rosenthal Affair.* New York: McCall Publishing, 1970.

Lynch, Dennis Tilden. *Criminals and Politicians.* New York: Macmillan Co., 1932.

McNamara, Joseph. *The Justice Story: True Tales of Murder, Mayhem and Mystery.* New York: Bannon Multi-Media Group, 2000.

Nash, Jay Robert. *World Encyclopedia of Organized Crime.* New York: Paragon House, 1992.

Nash, Jay Robert. *Bloodletters and Badmen: A Narrative Encyclopedia of American Criminals from the Pilgrims to the Present.* New York: M. Evans and Co., 1973.

Nelli, Humbert S. *The Business of Crime: Italians and Syndicate Crime in the United States.* New York: Oxford University Press, 1976.

Newell, Barbara Warne. *Chicago and the Labor Movement: Metropolitan Unionism in the 1930's.* Urbana, Ill.: University of Illinois Press, 1961.

O'Sullivan, Frank. *Gang Invasion of Business and Industry.* Chicago: O'Sullivan Publishing House, 1933.

Partridge, Eric. *A Dictionary of the Underworld.* New York: Macmillan Co., 1950.

Peterson, Virgil W. *The Mob: Two Hundred Years of Organized Crime in New York.* Ottawa, Ill.: Greenhill Publishers, 1983.

Powers, Richard Gid. *G-Men: Hoover's F.B.I. in Popular Culture.* Carbondale, Ill.: Southern Illinois University Press, 1983.

Reeve, Arthur. *The Golden Age of Crime.* New York: Mohawk Press, 1931.

Rockaway, Robert A. *But He Was Good to His Mother: The Lives and Crimes of Jewish Gangsters.* Jerusalem: Gefen Publishing House, 1993.

Sann, Paul. *Kill the Dutchman: The Story of Dutch Schultz.* New York: Arlington House, 1971.

Seidman, Harold. *The Labor Czars: A History of Labor Racketeering.* New York: Liveright Publishing Corporation, 1938.

Seidman, Joel. *The Needle Trades.* New York: Farrar and Rhinehart, 1942.

Smith, Brad. *Lawman to Outlaw: Verne Miller and the Kansas City Massacre.* Bedford, Ind.: Jona Books, 2002.

Smith, Richard Norton. *Thomas E. Dewey and His Times.* New York: Simon and Schuster, 1982.

Stolberg, Mary M. *Fighting Organized Crime: Politics, Justice and the Legacy of Thomas E. Dewey.* Boston: Northeastern University Press, 1995.

Summers, Anthony. *Official and Confidential: The Secret Life of J. Edgar Hoover.* New York: G. P. Putnam's Sons, 1993.

Sullivan, Edward Dean. *This Labor Union Racket.* New York: Hillman L. Curl, Inc., Publishers, 1936.

Terrett, Courtenay. *Only Saps Work: A Ballyhoo for Racketeering.* New York: Vanguard Press, 1931.

Thompson, Craig and Raymond Allen. *Gang Rule in New York: The Story of a Lawless Era.* New York: Dial Press, 1940.

Tully, Andrew. "The Lepke Era," in *Organized Crime in America,* Gus Tyler, ed. Ann Arbor: University of Michigan Press, 1962.

Turkus, Burton and Sid Feder. *Murder Inc.* New York: Farrar, Strauss and Young, 1951.

Tyler, Gus. *Organized Crime in America.* Ann Arbor, Mich.: University of Michigan Press, 1962.

Valentine, Lewis J. *Night Stick: The Autobiography of Lewis J. Valentine.* New York: Dial Press, 1947.

Walsh, George. *Public Enemies: The Mayor, the Mob and the Crime That Was.* New York: W. W. Norton, 1980.

Willemse, Cornelius. *Behind the Green Lights*. New York: Alfred A. Knopf, 1931.

Periodicals

"A.F.L. Ditches a Racketeer But Not Critics." *Life, 11*, October 27, 1941, 38-9.

"Business Prefers Racketeers." *New Republic*, Vol. 85, November 27, 1935.

"Case of Peter Panto." *Nation, 149*, September 16, 1939.

"Crime as a Profession." *American Mercury, 40*, February 1937.

"Crime in New York City." *Outlook Magazine, 98*, June 10, 1911.

"Days of Wickedness." *American Mercury, 12*, November 1927.

"Dealers in Death." *Reader's Digest, 28*, May 1936.

"Foreign Criminals in New York." *North American Review, 188*, September 1908.

"Gangs." *Atlantic Monthly, 141*, March 1928.

"Gangsters in the Dress Business." *Readers Digest, 67*, July 1955.

"Gunmen's Crimes in New York." *Independent, 82*, May 24, 1915.

"Halt of Racketeering." *Atlantic Monthly, 160*, October 1937.

"Hand in Your Pocket." *American Mercury, 122*, November 1936.

"How a Big City Breeds its Man Killers." *Harper's Magazine, 58*, June 13, 1914.

"How Murder Inc. Trains Killers." *American Mercury, 51*, October 1940.

"How New York Corrupts the East Side Boy." *Literary Digest, 45*, October 26, 1912.

"In the Days When New York Had its Gang Wars." *Literary Digest, 97*, June 9, 1928.

"Labor Racketeering." *The Nation, 137*, August 16, 1935.

"Labor Racketeers." *The Nation, 135*, July 27, 1932.

"Lepke: The Shy Boss of Murder Inc." *Life, 16*, February 28, 1944.

"Muscling in on Labor." *New Republic, 134*, April 30, 1950.

"Nemesis of Racketeers." *Literary Digest, 120*, November 30, 1935.

"New York Getting its Gunmen." *Literary Digest, 79*, December 15, 1923.

"New York, the Gunmen's Paradise." *Literary Digest, 79*, December 1, 1923.

"New York's Bad Men Not So Bad Now." *Literary Digest, 94,* August 6, 1927.

"New York's War on Rackets." *Collier's, 96,* October 5, 1935.

"Passing of the Gangster." *American Mercury, 4,* March 1925.

"Puzzle of the Underworld." *McClures, 41,* July 1913.

"Racketeering in the A.F.L." *The Nation, 141,* September 11, 18, 1935.

"Racketeers and Organized Labor." *Harper's Magazine, 161,* 1930.

"Racketeers Army of Punks." *Literary Digest, 114,* October 1, 1932.

"Racketeers." *New Republic, LXV 840,* January 7, 1931.

"Rackets and Labor." *Atlantic Monthly, 162,* September 1938.

"Rackets Can Be Routed." *Collier's, 104,* September 16, 1939.

"Reles' Retribution, Law of Gravity Finally Sends Singing 'Kid Twist' to His Grave." *Newsweek,* November 12, 1941.

"So I Joined the Union." *American Mercury, 44,* July 1938.

"Story of a Union and Underworld Ties." *U.S. News, 42,* March 8, 1957.

"Tammany's Control of New York by Professional Criminals." *McClure's Magazine,* Vol. 33, June 1909.

"The Business of Lawbreaking in New York." *Harper's Weekly, 52,* March 7, 1908.

"The Life of Lepke." *Newsweek ,* January 3, 1944.

"Unions vs. Racketeers." *U.S. News, 42,* February 1957.

"Using Gangs in Labor's Wars." *Literary Digest,* Vol. 50, 1260, May, 29, 1915.

"Wage Snatchers." *Readers Digest, 30,* March 1937.

"Waiting For Lepke." *Newsweek,* December 13, 1943.

"What We Learned About Labor Gangsters." *Saturday Evening Post, 230,* May 3, 10, 1958.

"When Clubs Were Trumps." *Outlook Magazine, 109,* April 7, 1915.

"Where the Gunmen Come From." *Outlook Magazine, 102,* November 30, 1912.

Adamic, Louis. "Racketeers and Organized Labor." *Harper's Magazine, 161.* 1930.

Asbury, Herbert. "The Passing of the Gangster." *American Mercury, 4,* March 1925.

Berger, Meyer. "Lepke: The Shy Boss of Murder Inc. Awaits Death in the Electric Chair." *Life,* February 28, 1944.

Champion, D. L. "Murder Inc. Homicides to Order." *True Detective,* July 1960.

Flynn, John T. "The Gangster in Business." *Colliers, 96,* October 5, 1935.

Goodman, Walter. "Muscling In On Labor." *New Republic, 134,* April 30, 1950.

Markey, Morris. "Gangs." *Atlantic Monthly,* Vol. 141, March 1928.

May, Allan. "The Last Days of 'Lepke' Buchalter." *Crime Magazine,* *http://crimemagazine.com/buchalter.htm.*

Preston, Francis. "Terror Racketeer." *Master Detective,* September 1940.

Stern, Michael. "Exposing New York's Racket Kings No, 2—Lepke and Gurrah." *True Detective Mysteries,* Vol. 29, October 1937.

Stern, Michael. "Inside Story of the $25,000 Dead or Alive Lepke Hunt." *True Detective Mysteries,* Vol. 33(2), November 1939.

Stern, Michael. "Smashing New York's Cut Rate Death Syndicate: Murder For Sale $5.00." *True Detective Mysteries,* July 1946.

Velic, Lester. "Gangsters in the Dress Business." *Reader's Digest, 67,* July 1953.

Newspapers
Atlanta Georgian
Boston Daily Record
Brooklyn Daily Eagle
Brooklyn Eagle
Buffalo (New York) *Evening News*
Detroit Free Press
Indianapolis Star
New Jersey Herald News
New York American
New York Daily Mirror
New York Daily News
New York Evening American
New York Journal-American
New York Herald Tribune
New York Post
New York Sun

Bibliography

New York Times
New York World-Telegram
Newark Ledger
Washington (D.C.) *Star*
Washington Post
Washington Times-Herald

Court Cases

289 N.Y. 181, 45 N.E. 2nd 225; *People v. Buchalter et al.*, Court of Appeals of New York, October 30, 1942, re-argument denied November 25, 1942.

Court of Appeals, Brooklyn, New York, People of the state of New York against Louis Buchalter, Emanuel Weiss, Louis Capone (May–June 1942), 1333–1347.

Court of General Sessions of the county of New York, Part V. People of the state of New York against Louis Buchalter, Max Silverman, Harold Silverman, Samuel Schorr (New York, January 26, 1940), vols. 1, 2, 3, and 4.

Court of General Sessions, People against Silverman, Silverman, and Schorr, 16; 12-13, 15.

People of the state of New York v. Lepke et al., 2103-2124.

Archival Papers
F.B.I. File 60-302.
F.B.I. File no. 60-1501.

Murder Inc. papers, Box 8; pp. 16-17, statement taken by Assistant District Attorney Solomon Klein, June 27, 1941; Morris Blustein questions, pp. 16-17, Municipal Archives of the City of New York.

O'Dwyer Papers, Brooklyn D.A. Files; Murder Inc., Box 10, p. 1; Memorandum of Information furnished by Albert Tannenbaum; Municipal Archives of the City of New York.

O'Dwyer Papers: Murder Inc., Box 7; Re: Louis Capone; Municipal Archives of the City of New York.

O'Dwyer Papers, Box 7; Memorandum of Information given by Albert Tannenbaum; Municipal Archives of the City of New York.

O'Dwyer Papers, Box 8; Memorandum of Information given by Albert Tannenbaum on June 5, 1941; re: cross exam of Charles

"Bug" Workman; Municipal Archives of the City of New York.

O'Dwyer Papers; Murder Inc., Box 7; Brooklyn D.A. Files; Municipal Archives of the City of New York.

O'Dwyer Papers; Murder Inc.; Brooklyn D.A. Files, Box 7; Memorandum of Information supplied by Sholem Bernstein; Municipal Archives of the City of New York.

O'Dwyer Papers; Murder Inc.; Brooklyn D.A. Files, Box 1; Case no. 16228, October 14, 1936; *The People v. John Doe*; testimony of Louis Stamler; Municipal Archives of the City of New York.

O'Dwyer Papers; Murder Inc.; Brooklyn D.A. Files, Box 1; Case no. 16228, October 14, 1936; *The People v. John Doe*; testimony of Officer Guglielmo Cappadora, 75th Precinct; Municipal Archives of the City of New York.

O'Dwyer Papers; Murder Inc.; Brooklyn D.A. Files, Box 1; Investigation into the death of Joseph Rosen; no. 16228; October 16, 1936, pp. 1-8; Municipal Archives of the City of New York.

O'Dwyer Papers; Murder Inc.; Brooklyn D.A. Files, Box 1; Police Department of the City of New York; resume of homicide case; Detective William S. King; September 13, 1936; File 18; Municipal Archives of the City of New York.

O'Dwyer Papers; Murder Inc.; Brooklyn D.A. Files, Box 1; statement no. 8565; statement taken in Woolworth Building, New York City (in office of Mr. Frank S. Hogan, Mr. Dewey's assistant), on December 16, 1937, commencing at about 2:25 P.M. by Assistant D.A. William E. McCarthy; pp. 1-3; Municipal Archives of the City of New York.

O'Dwyer Papers; Murder Inc.; Brooklyn D.A. Files, Box 1; testimony of Sholem Bernstein; pp. 10-32; Municipal Archives of the City of New York.

O'Dwyer Papers; Murder Inc.; Brooklyn D.A. Files, Box 10; In Regard Joseph Rosen Case, Abe Reles; Municipal Archives of the City of New York.

O'Dwyer Papers; Murder Inc.; Brooklyn D.A. Files, Box 10; *People v. Jack Parisi*; deposition taken by Burton B. Turkus, Esq., Assistant D.A., April 17, 1942; testimony of Albert Tannenbaum; pp 1-30; Municipal Archives of the City of New York.

O'Dwyer Papers; Murder Inc.; Brooklyn D.A. Files, Box 10; report regarding the investigation by this office in California, relating to the killing of Harry Greenberg alias "Big Greenie" alias Schacter; Municipal Archives of the City of New York.

O'Dwyer Papers; Murder Inc.; Brooklyn D.A. Files, Box 7; memorandum regarding the death of Whitey Friedman; Municipal Archives of the City of New York.

O'Dwyer Papers; Murder Inc.; Brooklyn D.A. Files, Box 8; Municipal Archives of the City of New York.

O'Dwyer papers; Murder Inc.; Brooklyn D.A. Files, Box 1; testimony of Esther Rosen, p. 16; Municipal Archives of the City of New York.

O'Dwyer papers; Murder Inc.; Brooklyn D.A. Files, Box 1; testimony of Harold Rosen, p. 9; statement no. 7229, October 5, 1936; Municipal Archives of the City of New York.

O'Dwyer Papers; Murder Inc. D.A. Files, Box 10; Julie Catalano deposition; 9-16; Municipal Archives of the City of New York.

O'Dwyer Papers; Murder Inc. files; *People of New York v. Nitzberg*; trial transcript, 154; Municipal Archives of the City of New York.

Endnotes

Chapter 1

1 Burton B. Turkus and Sid Feder, *Murder Inc.: The Story of the Syndicate* (New York: Farrar, Straus and Young, 1951), 331.

2 Meyer Berger, "Lepke: The Shy Boss of Murder Inc. Awaits Death in the Electric Chair," *Life* magazine, February 28, 1944, 86-87.

3 Albert Fried, *The Rise and Fall of the Jewish Gangster in America* (New York: Holt, Rinehart and Winston, 1980), 129.

4 "Lepke Receives New Sentence of 30 Years to Life," *New York World-Telegram*, April 6, 1940.

5 F.B.I. File no. 60-1501-980, Memorandum to the Director dated 1-28-38.

6 *The People of the State of New York v. Lepke et al.*, 2103-2124.

7 Jenna Weissman Joselit, *Our Gang: Jewish Crime and the New York Jewish Community 1900-1940* (Bloomington, Ind.: University of Indiana Press, 1987), 122.

8 Berger, *Life*, 1944, 87.

9 "Lepke Receives New Sentence of 30 Years to Life," *New York World-Telegram*, April 6, 1940.

10 Fried, *The Rise and Fall*, 130.

11 "How Lepke Became a Racket Czar," by Frank Doyle and William Falvey, *New York Daily Mirror*, April 27, 1940.

[12] Fried, *The Rise and Fall*, 131.

[13] "Gurrah Shapiro Dies While Doing Life Term," *New York Daily Mirror*, June 10, 1947.

[14] Leo Katcher, *The Big Bankroll: The Life and Times of Arnold Rothstein* (New York: Harper and Brothers, 1958, 1959), 283.

[15] Berger, *Life*, February 28, 1944.

[16] Turkus and Feder, *Murder Inc.*, 321.

[17] "Lepke a Gang Leader Who Liked His Privacy," by Foster Hailey, *New York Times*, V 10:1, August 13, 1939.

[18] Berger, *Life*, February 28, 1944, 87.

[19] F.B.I. File no. 601501-980: Memorandum to the Director dated 1-28-38. Background and activities of Louis Buchalter with aliases, 56.

[20] Turkus and Feder, *Murder Inc.*, 331.

[21] Fried, *The Rise and Fall*, 131-32.

Chapter 2

[1] Louis Adamic, "Racketeers and Organized Labor," *Harpers Magazine*, Vol. 161, 1930.

[2] Eric Partridge, *A Dictionary of the Underworld* (New York: Macmillan Co., 1950), 551-52.

[3] "Union Men Indicted in Gang Roundup," *New York Times*, Aug. 10, 1915.

[4] Hyman E. Goldin, ed., *Dictionary of American Underworld Lingo* (New York: Twayne Publishers, 1950), 173.

[5] Joselit, *Our Gang*, 106-107.

[6] Virgil W. Peterson, *The Mob: Two Hundred Years of Organized Crime in New York* (Ottawa, Ill.: Greenhill Publishers, 1983), 109-13.

[7] Joselit, *Our Gang*, 106-7.

[8] Barbara Warne Newell, *Chicago and the Labor Movement: Metropolitan Unionism in the 1930's* (Urbana, Ill.: University of Illinois Press, 1961), 79.

[9] Harold Seidman, *The Labor Czars: A History of Labor Racketeering* (New York: Liveright Publishing Corp., 1938), 45.

[10] "Tammany's Control of New York by Professional Criminals," *McClure's Magazine*, Vol. 33; June 1909, 123.

[11] Katcher, *The Big Bankroll*, 276.

[12] Rich Cohen, *Tough Jews: Fathers, Sons and Gangster Dreams* (New York: Simon and Schuster, 1998), 81.

13 "Monk Eastman and Coan Get Law's Limit," *New York Times,* April 20, 1904.

14 Herbert Asbury, *The Gangs of New York: An Informal History of the Underworld* (New York: Alfred Knopf, 1927), 286-7.

15 Fried, *The Rise and Fall,* 30-35.

16 Robert A. Rockaway, *But He Was Good to His Mother: The Lives and Crimes of Jewish Gangsters* (Jerusalem: Gefen Publishing House, 1993), 102.

17 Fried, *The Rise and Fall,* 32-33.

18 Katcher, *The Big Bankroll,* 276-77.

19 Andy Logan, *Against the Evidence: The Becker-Rosenthal Affair* (New York: McCall Publishing, 1970), 170-71.

20 Joselit, *Our Gang,* 107-8.

21 "Using Gangs in Labor's Wars," *Literary Digest,* Vol. 50, 1260, May 29, 1915.

22 Joselit, *Our Gang,* 106-7.

23 Fried, *The Rise and Fall,* 32-36.

24 "The Gangster Business," *New York Times,* May 16, 1915.

25 Cornelius Willemse, *Behind the Green Lights* (New York: Alfred A. Knopf, 1931), 290.

26 Joselit, *Our Gang,* 108.

27 Joselit, *Our Gang,* 108-10.

28 "Union Men Indicted in Gang Roundup," *New York Times,* August 10, 1915.

29 Willemse, *Behind the Green Lights,* 290.

30 Herbert Asbury, "The Passing of the Gangster," *American Mercury,* Vol. 4, March 1925, 360.

31 Joselit, *Our Gang,* 108-10.

32 Asbury, "The Passing of the Gangster," 311.

33 Morris Markey, "Gangs," *Atlantic Monthly,* Vol. 141, 296-305, March 1928.

34 Asbury, "The Passing of the Gangster," 361.

35 Joselit, *Our Gang,* 112.

36 Fried, *Rise and Fall,* 82-85.

37 "Union Men, He Says Killed Liebowitz," *New York Times,* September 25, 1915.

38 "7 Labor Leaders Face Murder Jury," *New York Times,* September 24, 1915.

39 Morris Hillquit, *Loose Leaves from a Busy Life* (New York: Macmillan

Co., 1934), 138-40.

[40] "Bury 'Little Augie,' Today Under Guard," *New York Times,* October 17, 1927.

Chapter 3

[1] Michael Stern, "Exposing New York's Racket Kings No. 2—Lepke and Gurrah," *True Detective Mysteries,* Vol. 29, October 1937, 38.

[2] Craig Thompson and Raymond Allen, *Gang Rule in New York: The Story of a Lawless Era* (New York: Dial Press, 1940), 228.

[3] Jay Robert Nash, *World Encyclopedia of Organized Crime* (New York: Paragon House, 1992), 314-15.

[4] J. Robert Kelly, *Encyclopedia of Organized Crime in the United States: From Capone's Chicago to the New Urban Underworld* (Westport, Conn.: Greenwood Press, 2000), 234.

[5] William Helmer, with Rick Mattix, *Public Enemies: America's Criminal Past 1919-1940* (New York: Check Mark Books, 1998), 36, 41, 81.

[6] Stern, "Exposing," 38-39.

[7] Markey, "Gangs," 296-305.

[8] Asbury, *The Gangs of New York,* 264, 369-370.

[9] "Gang Leader Slain at Courthouse Door as Police Guard Him," *New York Times,* August 29, 1923.

[10] Asbury, *The Gangs of New York,* 369-70.

[11] Willemse, *Behind the Green Lights,* 317-18.

[12] Stern, "Exposing," 37.

[13] Michael Stern, "The Inside Story of the 25,000 Dollar Dead or Alive Lepke Hunt," *True Detective Mysteries,* 1939.

[14] Asbury, *The Gangs of New York,* 370.

[15] "Fear New Gang War to Avenge Dropper," *New York Times,* August 30, 1923.

[16] Nash, 134-35.

[17] "Gang Leader Slain at Courthouse Door as Police Guard Him," *New York Times,* August 29, 1923.

[18] Asbury, *The Gangs of New York,* 370-375.

[19] *New York Times,* August 29, 1923.

[20] Asbury, *The Gangs of New York,* 370-375.

[21] Stern, "The Inside Story," 119.

[22] "Dropper Is Buried; His Slayer Indicted," *New York Times,* August 31, 1923.

23 "Arraign 3 as Gangsters," *New York Times,* Sept. 6, 1923.

24 Thompson and Allen, *Gang Rule,* 252.

25 Fried, *The Rise and Fall,* 136.

26 Thompson and Allen, *Gang Rule,* 227.

27 Fried, *The Rise and Fall,* 136-37.

28 Thompson and Allen, *Gang Rule,* 230-31.

29 Joselit, *Our Gang,* 118-20.

30 Seidman, *The Labor Czars,* 118-19.

31 Fried, *The Rise and Fall,* 138.

32 Joselit, *Our Gang,* 115-20.

33 Fried, *The Rise and Fall,* 140-41.

34 Thompson and Allen, *Gang Rule,* 233-35.

35 Katcher, *The Big Bankroll,* 284.

36 Fried, *The Rise and Fall,* 140-41.

37 Thompson and Allen, *Gang Rule,* 233-35.

38 "Gangsters Give Up in Killing," *New York Times,* Oct. 20, 1927.

39 Peterson, *The Mob: Two Hundred Years,* 147-49.

Chapter 4

1 Peterson, *The Mob: Two Hundred Years,* 147-49.

2 Turkus and Feder, *Murder Inc.,* 144.

3 "Little Augie Slain by Rival Gangsters," *New York Times,* October 16, 1927.

4 Stern, "Exposing."

5 Asbury, *The Gangs of New York,* 373.

6 "Gangsters Mourn as 'Little Augie' is Buried," *New York Times,* October 18, 1927.

7 "Gangsters Give Up," *New York Times,* October 27, 1927.

8 Stern, "Exposing."

9 Berger, "Lepke," 86.

10 Turkus and Feder, *Murder Inc.,* 33.

11 Berger, "Lepke," 86.

12 "Business Prefers Racketeers," *New Republic,* Vol. 85, November 27, 1935, 69.

13 Berger, "Lepke," 86-98.

14 Richard Hammer, *Playboy's Illustrated History of Organized Crime* (Chicago: Playboy Press, 1975), 184.

15 Gus Tyler, *Organized Crime in America* (Ann Arbor, Mich.: University of Michigan Press, 1962), 207.

[16] Stern, "Exposing," 100.

[17] Daniel Allen Hearn, *Legal Executions in New York State 1639-1963* (Jefferson, N.C.: McFarland & Co., 1997), 243.

[18] Block, *Eastside Westside*, 168-183.

[19] Block, *Eastside Westside*, 171.

Chapter 5

[1] Stern, *True Detective Mysteries,* Oct. 1937, 100.

[2] Sen. Royal S. Copeland, New York, August 14, 1932.

[3] Block, *Eastside Westside*, 76.

[4] Joel Seidman, *The Needle Trades* (New York: Farrar and Rhinehart, 1942), 190-191.

[5] Mary M. Stolberg, *Fighting Organized Crime: Politics, Justice and the Legacy of Thomas E. Dewey* (Boston: Northeastern University Press, 1995), 161-165.

[6] Turkus and Feder, *Murder Inc.,* 338-343.

[7] Turkus and Feder, *Murder Inc.,* 338-343.

[8] Stephen Fox, *Blood and Power: Organized Crime in Twentieth Century America* (New York: William Morrow, 1989), 213-217.

[9] Thomas E. Dewey, *Twenty Against the Underworld* (Garden City: Doubleday, 1974), 176.

[10] Fox, *Blood and Power,* 218.

[11] Turkus and Feder, *Murder Inc.,* 352.

[12] Stolberg, *Fighting Organized Crime,* 165.

[13] John Hutchinson, *The Imperfect Union: A History of Corruption in American Trade Unions* (New York: E. P. Dutton, 1970), 76.

[14] Court of Appeals, Brooklyn, New York, *The People of the State of New York Against Louis Buchalter, Emanuel Weiss, Louis Capone* (May-June 1942), 1333-1347.

[15] Stern, "Inside Story," 121.

[16] Murder, Inc. papers, Box 8; pp. 16-17, statement taken by Assistant District Attorney Solomon Klein, June 27, 1941; Morris Blustein questions, pp. 16-17; Municipal Archives of the City of New York.

[17] Stern, "Exposing,"120-122.

[18] Block, *Eastside Westside*, 173-174.

[19] Fried, *The Rise and Fall*, 157-160.

[20] "Acid Spilled on Fur Dealer Put an Eye Out," *New York World-Telegram,* Oct. 29, 1936.

[21] "Fur Racketeer Blinded Him, Says Witness," *New York American,*

Oct. 30, 1936.

22 Fried, *The Rise and Fall*, 157-160.

23 Stern, "Exposing,"121.

24 "Fur Terrorism Described," *Newark Ledger,* Nov. 17, 1937.

25 Stern, "Exposing," 121.

26 Howard Abadansky, *Organized Crime* (Chicago: Nelson-Hill, 1997), 101.

27 John McNulty, "Fatal Fur Raid Told by Felon," *New York Daily Mirror,* November 3, 1936.

28 "158 Are Indicted in Fur Rackets," *Washington* (D.C.) *Star,* Nov. 11, 1933.

29 Dewey, *Twenty Against*, 309.

30 Block, *Eastside Westside*, 169.

31 Court of General Sessions of the County of New York, Part V. *The People of the State of New York Against Louis Buchalter, Max Silverman, Harold Silverman, Samuel Schorr* (New York, January 26, 1940), Vols. 1, 2, 3, and 4.

32 Dewey, *Twenty Against*, 298.

33 Dewey, *Twenty Against*, 298.

34 Court of General Sessions, *The People Against Silverman, Silverman, and Schorr*, 16; 12-13, 15.

35 Rupert Hughes, *Attorney for the People: The Story of Thomas Dewey* (New York: Houghton Mifflin, 1940), 119.

36 "Sang on Lepke, Gets Light Term," *New York Daily Mirror,* July 1, 1941.

Chapter 6

1 Turkus and Feder, *Murder Inc.*, 346.

2 Turkus and Feder, *Murder Inc.*

3 Richard Norton Smith, *Thomas E. Dewey and His Times* (New York: Simon and Schuster, 1982), 221.

4 "Racket Chief Slain After 18 Attempts," *New York Times,* September 18, 1931.

5 "How Murder Inc. Trains Killers," *American Mercury,* Vol. 51, October 1940.

6 "Gunman Tells How Gang Killed Rudack, 'Fighting Jeweler,'" *New York Times,* August 28, 1926.

7 "Gunmen in Break All Deep in Crime," *New York Times,* November 4, 1926.

[8] "Four Die, Three Shot in Tombs Battle as Gunfire Halts Jail Break," November 4, 1926.

[9] "Two Seized in Plot to Escape Tombs; 4 Inquiries Ordered," *New York Times*, November 5, 1926.

[10] Edward Dean Sullivan, *This Labor Union Racket* (New York: Hillman L. Curl, Inc., Publishers, 1936), 36-46.

[11] Rockaway, *But He Was Good*, 22.

[12] "7th Killing is Laid to Fear Mad Thug," *New York Times*, October 24, 1935.

[13] Block, *Eastside Westside*, 221.

[14] "Racket Chief Slain After 18 Attempts," *New York Times*, September 18, 1931.

[15] "Murder of Three Brothers Solved as Reles Squeals on Killers," *Brooklyn Eagle*, April 6, 1940.

[16] "Reles' Retribution, Law of Gravity Finally Sends Singing 'Kid Twist' to His Grave," *Newsweek*, November 12, 1941.

[17] Block, *Eastside Westside*, 223.

[18] "How Murder Inc. Trains Killers," *American Mercury*, Vol. 51, October 1940.

[19] John H. Davis, *Mafia Dynasty: The Rise and Fall of the Gambino Crime Family* (New York: HarperCollins, 1993), 52-53.

[20] D. L. Champion, "Murder Inc. Homicides to Order," *True Detective*, July 1960.

[21] O'Dwyer Papers: Murder Inc., Box 7; Re: Louis Capone; Municipal Archives of the City of New York.

[22] Michael Stern, "Smashing New York's Cut Rate Death Syndicate: Murder For Sale $5.00," *True Detective Mysteries*, July 1946.

[23] Turkus and Feder, *Murder Inc.*, 350.

[24] O'Dwyer Papers; Murder Inc. files; *People of New York v. Nitzberg*; trial transcript, 154; Municipal Archives of the City of New York.

[25] Turkus and Feder, *Murder Inc.*, xi.

Chapter 7

[1] Champion, "Homicides to Order," 64-65.

[2] Turkus and Feder, *Murder Inc.*, 348.

[3] F.B.I. File no. 60-1501-980.

[4] F.B.I. File no. 60-1501-4266.

[5] Berger, "Lepke: The Shy Boss of Murder Inc. Awaits Death in the Electric Chair," *Life Magazine*, February 28, 1944, 88-90.

6 F.B.I. File no. 60-1501-2774.

7 Stolberg, *Fighting Organized Crime*, 165.

8 O'Dwyer Papers, Box 7; Memorandum of Information given by Albert Tannenbaum; Municipal Archives of the City of New York.

9 Stern, "Inside Story," 120-22.

10 O'Dwyer Papers, Box 8; Memorandum of Information given by Albert Tannenbaum on June 5, 1941; re: cross exam of Charles "Bug" Workman; Municipal Archives of the City of New York.

11 F.B.I. File no. 60-1501-304.

Chapter 8

1 Brad Smith, *Lawman to Outlaw: Verne Miller and the Kansas City Massacre* (Bedford, Ind.: JoNa Books, 2002), 43-55.

2 Fox, *Blood and Power*, 158-170.

3 Dewey, *Twenty Against*, 149-150.

4 Fox, *Blood and Power*, 204.

5 Dewey, *Twenty Against*, 205.

6 Elmer L. Irey, as told to William J. Slocum, *The Tax Dodgers: The Inside Story of the T-Men's War with America's Political and Underworld Hoodlums* (New York: Greenberg Publishing Co., 1948).

7 John T. Flynn, "The Gangster in Business," *Collier's*, Vol. 96, Oct. 5, 1933.

8 George Walsh, *Public Enemies: The Mayor, the Mob, and the Crime That Was* (New York: W. W. Norton and Co., 1980), 68.

9 Peterson, *The Mob: 200 Years*, 204.

10 Flynn, "The Gangster in Business," 15.

11 Hughes, *Attorney for the People*, 65.

12 Fox, *Blood and Power*, 158-170.

13 Thompson and Raymond, *Gang Rule*, 252-260.

14 Paul Sann, *Kill the Dutchman: The Story of Dutch Schultz* (New York: Arlington House, 1971), 277.

15 Turkus and Feder, *Murder Inc.*, 128-149.

16 Sann, *Kill the Dutchman*, 276-280.

17 Martin A. Gosch and Richard Hammer, *The Last Testament of Lucky Luciano* (Boston: Little Brown, 1974), 193-197.

18 Turkus and Feder, *Murder Inc.*, 214.

19 "34 Face for Racket Trial Monday," *New York American,* October 24, 1936.

20 "Two Go on Trial for Racket Case," *New York Times*, October 27, 1936.

[21] "Lepke-Gurrah Trial Goes to Jury Today," *New York American,* November 6, 1936.

[22] "U.S. to Open New Racket Drive Today," *New York American,* November 9, 1936.

[23] "Lepke and Gurrah Get Two Years Each," *New York World-Telegram,* November 12, 1936.

[24] "No Bail," *New York World-Telegram,* November 14, 1936.

[25] Smith, *Thomas E. Dewey and His Times,* 223.

[26] "Bail for Convicted Big Shots," *New York World-Telegram,* December 5, 1936.

[27] "Fur Racketeers Slip Out on Bail," *New York Post,* December 4, 1936.

[28] Smith, *Thomas E. Dewey and His Times,* 282.

[29] Turkus and Feder, *Murder Inc.,* 217.

[30] Thompson and Raymond, *Gang Rule,* 252-260.

[31] Peterson, *The Mob,* 218.

[32] Charles Garrett, *The LaGuardia Years* (New Brunswick, N.J.: Rutgers University Press, 1961), 170.

[33] F.B.I. file no. 60-1501-3222X.

[34] Hammer, *Playboy's Illustrated History,* 185.

[35] Andrew Tully, "The Lepke Era," in *Organized Crime in America,* Gus Tyler, ed. (Ann Arbor: University of Michigan Press, 1962), 210.

[36] George Caroll, "Lepke Sank Fortune in Big Dope Ring," *New York Journal-American,* August 8, 1939.

[37] Stern, "Inside Story," 122.

[38] Tully, "The Lepke Era," 209-211.

[39] "Girls Worked in Lepke Dope Ring, Jury Told," *New York Daily News,* December 1, 1937.

[40] "Bare Lepke's Girl Tourists in Dope Ring," *New York Daily News,* December 1, 1937.

[41] "Four Men Sentenced as Narcotics Smugglers," *Washington Star,* November 28, 1938.

[42] "When the Federal Men Get Busy," Passaic, New Jersey *Herald News,* April 18, 1938.

[43] "Prosecutors Seek Life Term for Gurrah," *Brooklyn Daily Eagle,* April 16, 1938.

[44] "'Gurrah' Pleads Not Guilty, But Woes Pile Up," *New York Herald Tribune,* April 16, 1938.

[45] "$25,000 'Fix' in Labor Murder," *New York Daily Mirror,* July 2, 1938.

46 Hughes, *Attorney for the People*, 120-123.

47 "'Gurrah' Gets 3 Years, Weeps, Protests That He Was Framed," *New York Herald Tribune*, June 18, 1938.

48 "'Gurrah,' Guilty, Faces Five Years," *New York Post*, June 18, 1938.

Chapter 9

1 Hammer, *Playboy's Illustrated History*, 183-187.

2 Francis Preston, "Terror Racketeer," *Master Detective*, September 1940, 69.

3 Turkus and Feder, *Murder Inc.*, 357

4 "U.S. Refuses to Give Lepke to Dewey," *New York Herald Tribune*, August 26, 1939.

5 William O'Dwyer Papers; Murder Inc., Box 7; Brooklyn D.A. Files; Municipal Archives of the City of New York.

6 F.B.I. File 60-302, 4-15.

7 Turkus and Feder, *Murder Inc.*, 352.

8 "50 Police Detailed to Lepke Search," *New York Times*, August 4, 1939.

9 Lewis J. Valentine, *Night Stick: The Autobiography of Lewis J. Valentine, Former Police Commissioner of New York City* (New York: Dial Press, 1947), 137.

10 "U.S. Raises Price on Lepke to $50,000," *Detroit Free Press*, August 23, 1939.

11 Richard Gid Powers, *G-Men: Hoover's F.B.I. in Popular Culture* (Carbondale, Ill.: Southern Illinois University Press, 1983), 182-83.

12 Kenneth T. Jackson and John B. Manbock, *The Neighborhoods of Brooklyn* (New Haven and London: Yale University Press, 1998), 41.

13 F.B.I. File 60-302, 16-17.

14 "Gang Killer Used Garb of Woman," *New York Times*, April 21, 1940.

15 William O'Dwyer Papers; Murder Inc.; D.A. Files, Box 10; Julie Catalano deposition; 9-16; Municipal Archives of the City of New York.

16 F.B.I. File 60-302, 17-206.

17 Patrick Downey, *Gangster City: The History of the New York Underworld 1900-1935* (New Jersey: Barricade Books, 2004), 174.

18 F.B.I. File 60-302, 51-65.

[19] Stern, "The Inside Story."

[20] Harry J. Anslinger, with Will Oursler, *The Murderers: The Shocking Story of the Narcotics Gangs* (New York: Farrar, Straus and Cudahy, 1961), 49-50.

[21] Tully, "The Lepke Era," 208.

[22] Turkus and Feder, *Murder Inc.,* 387.

[23] Al Binder and John McNulty, "Seek Ex-Schoolmaster to Send Lepke to Chair," *New York Daily News,* April 17, 1940.

[24] "Lepke Aide, Long Missing, is Found Slain; O'Dwyer Follows Trail to Sullivan County," *New York Times,* April 16, 1940.

[25] William O'Dwyer Papers; Murder Inc.; Brooklyn D.A. Files, Box 7; Memorandum of Information supplied by Sholem Bernstein; Municipal Archives of the City of New York.

[26] Preston, "Terror Racketeer," 43.

[27] Stern, "Inside Story," 124-25.

[28] William O'Dwyer Papers, Brooklyn D.A. Files; Murder Inc., Box 10, p. 1; Memorandum of Information furnished by Albert Tannenbaum; Municipal Archives of the City of New York.

[29] Dewey, *Twenty Against,* 309.

[30] Block, *Eastside Westside,* 169.

[31] Stern, "The Inside Story," 125-27.

[32] William O'Dwyer Papers; Murder Inc.; Brooklyn D.A. Files, Box 7; memorandum regarding the death of Whitey Friedman; Municipal Archives of the City of New York.

[33] Turkus and Feder, *Murder Inc.,* 180-86.

[34] "O'Dwyer on Trail of Schultz Killer," *New York Times,* April 4, 1940.

[35] William O'Dwyer Papers; Murder Inc.; Brooklyn D.A. Files, Box 8; Municipal Archives of the City of New York.

[36] William O'Dwyer Papers; Murder Inc.; Brooklyn D.A. Files, Box 10; *People v. Jack Parisi*; deposition taken by Burton B. Turkus, Esq., Assistant D.A., April 17, 1942; testimony of Albert Tannenbaum; pp 1-30; Municipal Archives of the City of New York.

[37] Preston, "Terror Racketeer," 48.

[38] "Terror Reign Seen Snared Gangs," *Brooklyn Eagle,* March 27, 1940.

[39] "Gang Money-Man, Thought Murdered Appears in Court," *Brooklyn Eagle,* April 15, 1940.

[40] Turkus and Feder, *Murder Inc.,* 355.

[41] "Brooklyn Hideout of Lepke Revealed," *New York Times,* April 13, 1940.

42 F.B.I. File 60-302, 31-50.

43 Gosch and Hammer, *The Last Testament*, 240-45.

44 Turkus and Feder, *Murder Inc.*, 350-60.

45 "Capture of Lepke Made by Winchell," *Boston Daily Record*, August 26, 1939.

46 "Lepke Surrender Arranged by Winchell," *Atlanta Georgian*, August 26, 1939.

47 Turkus and Feder, *Murder Inc.*, 350-66.

48 Turkus and Feder, *Murder Inc.*, 360-61.

49 "Capture of Lepke Made by Winchell."

50 "Lepke Surrenders to F.B.I.; Racketeer Never Left City," *New York Times*, August 25, 1939.

51 F.B.I. Keeps Lepke from Dewey Aides," *New York Times*, August 26, 1939.

52 "Narcotics Suspect Held," *New York Times*, September 3, 1939.

53 "Five Found Guilty of Aiding Lepke," *New York Times*, November 7, 1939.

54 "New Indictment Names Lepke and Silvermans," *New York Herald Tribune*, November 3, 1939.

55 Turkus and Feder, *Murder Inc.*, 270-80.

56 William O'Dwyer Papers; Murder Inc.; Brooklyn D.A. Files, Box 10; report regarding the investigation by this office in California, relating to the killing of Harry Greenberg alias "Big Greenie" alias Schacter; Municipal Archives of the City of New York.

57 "Hollywood Slaying Called Gang Revenge," *New York Times*, November 24, 1939.

58 William O'Dwyer Papers; Murder Inc.; Brooklyn D.A. Files, Box 10; report regarding the investigation by this office in California, relating to the killing of Harry Greenberg alias "Big Greenie" alias Schacter; Municipal Archives of the City of New York.

59 "Hollywood Slaying Called Gang Revenge."

60 "Gangster Slain on Coast, a Lepke Aide; Once Deported, He Slipped Back into the U.S.," *New York Times*, November 25, 1939.

Chapter 10

1 Dean Jennings, *We Only Kill Each Other: The Life and Bad Times of Bugsy Siegel* (Englewood Cliffs, N.J.: Prentice-Hall, 1967), 85.

2 "Gangster Brought to Book," *Indianapolis Star*, December 22, 1939.

3 "Court Will Hear How Lepke Aide Bared Dope Ring," *New York*

Daily Mirror, December 1, 1939.

[4] "Lepke Pictured as Cutting in on Smugglers," *New York Herald Tribune,* December 1, 1939.

[5] "Lepke Witness Bares Big Profit," *New York Times,* December 2, 1939.

[6] "Narcotics Leader Identifies Lepke," *New York Times,* December 7, 1939.

[7] "2 Witnesses Link Lepke to Ring," *New York Times,* December 13, 1939.

[8] "Mob Victim Found in N.J. Identified as Lepke Fugitive," *New York Daily News,* December 12, 1939.

[9] "Government Ends Lepke Testimony," *New York Times,* December 14, 1939.

[10] "Myth About Lepke Assailed at Trial," *New York Times,* December 20, 1939.

[11] "Lepke is Convicted in Narcotics Case," *New York Times,* December 27, 1939.

[12] "U.S. 'Lends' Lepke to Dewey for Trial," *New York Daily News,* January 3, 1940.

[13] "Lepke is Handed Over," *New York Herald Tribune,* January 4, 1940.

[14] "Dewey Will Get Lepke Today on Racket Charges," *New York Herald Tribune,* January 4, 1940.

[15] "Lepke is Mute in State Court," *New York Sun,* January 4, 1940.

[16] "50 Counts Facing Lepke, Five Others in Garment Racket," *Washington Times-Herald,* January 6, 1940.

[17] "Dismiss Lepke's Writ to Avoid Racket Trial," *New York Daily News,* January 6, 1940.

[18] "Buchalter Loses Fight to Avoid State Charges," *Washington Post,* June 6, 1940.

[19] "Lepke Accused in Garment Racket," *Buffalo* (New York) *Evening News,* January 17, 1940.

[20] "Lepke May Have to Serve 554 Yr. Term," *New York Daily Mirror,* January 17, 1940.

[21] "Lepke Receives Jolt as Goldis Pleads Guilty," *New York Sun,* January 24, 1940.

[22] "Lepke Stunned as Pal Goldis Admits Guilt," *New York Journal-American,* January 24, 1940.

[23] "Lepke Victim Swears He Paid Thousands," *New York Daily Mirror,* February 8, 1940.

24 "Schorr Deserts Lepke," *New York Journal-American*, February 7, 1940.

25 "Aide of Lepke Says He Paid Solomon Cut," *New York Herald Tribune*, February 13, 1940.

26 "Shot Week After Telling on Lepke," *New York Daily Mirror*, February 14, 1940.

27 "Another Hard One for Tammany," *New York World-Telegram*, February 14, 1940.

28 "Lepke's Link to Solomon Aired at Trial," *New York Sun*, February 15, 1940.

29 "State Rests Case in Trial of Lepke," *New York Times*, February 17, 1940.

30 "Lepke Gets Life in Extortion Case," *New York Times Herald*, March 2, 1940.

31 "Lepke Sentenced to Thirty Years to Life," *New York Times*, April 6, 1940.

Chapter 11

1 "Sang on Lepke, Gets Light Term," *New York Daily Mirror*, July 1, 1941.

2 Turkus and Feder, *Murder Inc.*, 375.

3 O'Dwyer Papers; Murder Inc.; Brooklyn D.A. Files, Box 1; Case no. 16228, October 14, 1936; *The People v. John Doe*; testimony of Louis Stamler; Municipal Archives of the City of New York.

4 O'Dwyer Papers; Murder Inc.; Brooklyn D.A. Files, Box 1; Case no. 16228, October 14, 1936; *The People v. John Doe*; testimony of Officer Guglielmo Cappadora, 75th Precinct; Municipal Archives of the City of New York.

5 O'Dwyer Papers; Murder Inc.; Brooklyn D.A. Files, Box 1; Police Department of the City of New York; resume of homicide case; Detective William S. King; September 13, 1936; File 18; Municipal Archives of the City of New York.

6 Turkus and Feder, *Murder Inc.*, 61-62.

7 "Reles Links Lepke to Murder for Hire," *New York Times*, April 14, 1940.

8 O'Dwyer Papers; Murder Inc.; Brooklyn D.A. Files, Box 10; In Regard Joseph Rosen Case, Abe Reles; Municipal Archives of the City of New York.

9 "Two Lepke Aides Face Court Today," *New York Times*, May 28, 1940.

10 "Official of Union Linked to Murder," *New York Post,* September 21, 1936.

11 O'Dwyer Papers; Murder Inc.; Brooklyn D.A. Files, Box 1; statement no. 8565; statement taken in Woolworth Building, New York City (in office of Mr. Frank S. Hogan, Mr. Dewey's assistant), on December 16, 1937, commencing at about 2:25 P.M. by Assistant D.A. William E. McCarthy; pp. 1-3; Municipal Archives of the City of New York.

12 Turkus and Feder, *Murder Inc.,* 388-89.

13 289 N.Y. 181, 45 N.E. 2nd 225; *People v. Buchalter et al.,* Court of Appeals of New York, October 30, 1942, re-argument denied November 25, 1942.

14 "Slain Man's Kin Names Shapiro in Lepke Trial," *Brooklyn Eagle,* October 23, 1941.

15 O'Dwyer Papers; Murder Inc.; Brooklyn D.A. Files, Box 1; Investigation into the death of Joseph Rosen; no. 16228; October 16, 1936, pp. 1-8; Municipal Archives of the City of New York.

16 289 N.Y. 181, 45 N.E. 2nd 225; *People v. Buchalter et al.,* Court of Appeals of New York, October 30, 1942, re-argument denied November 25, 1942.

17 O'Dwyer Papers; Murder Inc.; Brooklyn D.A. Files; Box 1; statement taken in Woolworth Building, New York City (in office of Frank S. Hogan, Mr. Dewey's assistant), December 16, 1937; commencing at about 2:25 P.M. by Assistant D.A. William E. McCarthy; Municipal Archives of the City of New York.

18 Turkus and Feder, *Murder Inc.,* 373.

19 289 N.Y. 181, 45 N.E. 2nd 225; *People v. Buchalter et al.,* Court of Appeals of New York, October 30, 1942, re-argument denied November 25, 1942.

20 Turkus and Feder, Murder Inc. 375.

21 289 N.Y. 181, 45 N.E. 2nd 225; *People v. Buchalter et al.,* Court of Appeals of New York, October 30, 1942, re-argument denied November 25, 1942, 14.

22 "Lepke Aide, Long Missing, Is Found Slain; O'Dwyer Follows Trail to Sullivan County," *New York Times,* April 16, 1940.

23 O'Dwyer Papers; Murder Inc.; Brooklyn D.A. Files, Box 1; testimony of Sholem Bernstein; pp. 10-32; Municipal Archives of the City of New York.

24 "Asks U.S. Grant to Try Lepke," *New York Sun,* May 28, 1940.

25 "O'Dwyer Off to Get Lepke for Trial," *New York Times*, September 21, 1940.

26 "Lepke Henchman Captured Here," *New York World-Telegram*, November 30, 1940.

27 "Lepke Offered Second Deal to Beat Chair," *New York Journal-American*, January 31, 1941.

28 "Lepke's Ally Gets 10 Years as Dope Seller," *New York Daily News*, February 5, 1941.

29 Turkus and Feder, *Murder Inc.*, 369.

30 "Lepke Aide Slain As He Minds Baby in a Flat in Bronx," *New York Times*, February 7, 1941.

31 "Lepke Aide Slain in Bronx," *New York Post*, February 7, 1941.

32 "'Ben the Boss,' Lepke Aide, Slain to Cover Up 3 Gang Murders," *New York Daily Mirror*, February 8, 1941.

33 "Murder Suspect in Ring Held Here," *New York Times*, April 13, 1941.

34 "Lepke Aide Slain as U.S. Corrals Gang; He Knew Too Much," *New York Daily News*, April 18, 1941.

35 "Gangster Slain after Indictment for Hiding Fugitive Buchalter," *New York Daily News*, April 18, 1941.

36 "Writ Orders U.S. Surrender Lepke," *New York Daily Mirror*, April 30, 1941.

37 "Judge Hits 'Armed Arsenal' of 47 Guarding Lepke Here," *Brooklyn Eagle*, May 9, 1941.

38 "Lepke Asks Permission to Finish Prison Term," *Brooklyn Eagle*, June 11, 1941.

39 "O'Dwyer to Tell Basis of Lepke Charge Today," *New York Evening American*, June 16, 1941.

40 "Capone Denied Separate Trial in Rosen Murder," *Brooklyn Eagle*, June 20, 1941.

41 "Lepke Must Face Murder Trial Now," *Brooklyn Eagle*, June 20, 1941.

42 "Lepke Trial Opens; Jury-Picking Lags," *New York Times*, August 5, 1941.

43 "Talesman Balky, Lepke Trial Off Until September 15," *New York Journal American*, August 5, 1941.

44 "Lepke Trial Opens, Hard to Get Jury," *New York Times*, September 16, 1941.

45 "Lepke Jury Filled After Five Weeks," *New York Times*, October 18, 1941.

[46] "Widow Accuses Aide of Lepke," *New York Times,* October 21, 1941.

[47] O'Dwyer Papers; Murder Inc.; Brooklyn D.A. Files, Box 1; testimony of Esther Rosen, p. 16; Municipal Archives of the City of New York.

[48] "Murdered Man's Son Puts Finger on Lepke," *Brooklyn Eagle,* October 22, 1941.

[49] "Son of Slain Witness Heard at Lepke Trial," *New York Times,* October 23, 1941.

[50] O'Dwyer Papers; Murder Inc.; Brooklyn D.A. Files, Box 1; testimony of Harold Rosen, p. 9; statement no. 7229, October 5, 1936; Municipal Archives of the City of New York.

[51] "Flight of Slayers Described in Court," *New York Times,* October 22, 1941.

[52] "Slain Rosen's Daughter Tells of Lepke Visit," *New York Herald Tribune,* October 24, 1941.

[53] "Rosen's Daughter Also Names Lepke," *New York Daily News,* October 24, 1941.

[54] "Lepke Witness Tells of Murder Rule Training," *New York Herald Tribune,* October 25, 1941.

[55] "'Rat' Tells of Job in Murder Ring," *New York Times,* October 28, 1941.

[56] "Experts Stomped by 'Shlem' Job," *Brooklyn Eagle,* October 30, 1941.

[57] "Aide Links Lepke to Rosen Slaying," *New York Times,* November 1, 1941.

[58] "'Burn Lepke' Pledge Denied by Max Rubin," *New York Times,* November 6, 1941.

[59] "Raging Witness Sets Lepke Case in Uproar," *New York Times,* November 7, 1941.

[60] "Lepke Aide Tells of Murder Plots," *New York Times,* November 8, 1941.

[61] "Reles Dies in Hotel Plunge as Escape Attempt Fails," *Brooklyn Eagle,* November 12, 1941.

[62] Gosch and Hammer, *The Last Testament,* 251-255.

[63] Turkus and Feder, *Murder Inc.,* 390-92.

[64] "Roommate Shaken by Death of Reles," *New York Times,* November 13, 1941.

[65] "Tells of Sluggings," *New York Times,* November 14, 1941.

66 Turkus and Feder, *Murder Inc.*, 390-96.

67 "Pistol User Says He Balks at Lies," *New York Times*, November 16, 1941.

68 Turkus and Feder, *Murder Inc.*, 393-96.

69 "State Rests Case in Lepke Trial," *New York Times*, November 18, 1941.

70 Turkus and Feder, *Murder Inc.*, 379.

71 "Lepke Witness Tries 'Walkout,'" *New York Times*, November 19, 1941.

72 Turkus and Feder, *Murder Inc.*, 401.

73 "Gurrah Arrives for Lepke Trial," *New York Times*, November 20, 1941.

74 "Lepke Aide's Alibi is Birthday Party," *New York Times*, November 22, 1941.

75 "Lepke was Framed His Counsel Asserts," *New York Times*, November 27, 1941.

76 "Lepke Convicted With Two Aides; All Face Death," *New York Times*, November 30, 1941.

Chapter 12

1 Turkus and Feder, *Murder Inc.*, 406.

2 "Lepke and 2 Aides Sentenced to Die," *New York Times*, December 3, 1941.

3 "Boro Killers Hustled Off to Death House," *Brooklyn Eagle*, December 3, 1941.

4 "Lepke's Fate Put Up to President by Death Verdict," *New York Times*, December 1, 1941.

5 H. Paul Jeffers, *Gentleman Gerald* (New York: St. Martin's Press, 1995), 43-45.

6 Robert Hayden Alcorn, *The Count of Gramercy Park: The Story of Gerald Chapman, Gangster* (London: Hurst and Blackett, 1955), 198-99.

7 Turkus and Feder, *Murder Inc.*, 408.

8 "Lepke to Exhaust All Legal Appeals," *New York Times*, December 2, 1941.

9 "Lepke Plans Appeal to U.S. Supreme Court," *Brooklyn Eagle*, December 1, 1941.

10 "White House Action May Be Required to Execute Lepke," *Washington Star*, December 1, 1941.

11 "Lepke to Take Fight for Life to High Court," *New York Daily*

Mirror, December 1, 1941.

12 "Lepke Conviction Upheld in Albany," *New York Times,* October 31, 1942.

13 "Lepke, 2 Aides Win Stay of Execution," *New York Times,* December 6, 1942.

14 "Lepke Execution Stayed," *New York Times,* January 3, 1943.

15 "Lepke's Last Hope Revived by Court," *New York Times,* March 16, 1943.

16 "High Court Seals Lepke Trio Deaths," *New York Times,* June 2, 1943.

17 "Biddle is Urged to Free Lepke so Slayer Can Be Put to Death," *New York Times,* July 10, 1943.

18 "U.S. Still Refuses to Release Lepke," *New York Times,* July 16, 1943.

19 "State Wins Fight to Sentence Lepke," *New York Times,* July 17, 1943.

20 "Lepke Again Hears Death Sentence," *New York Times,* July 21, 1943.

21 "Dewey Demands Lepke's Surrender," *New York Times,* September 2, 1943.

22 "Dewey Gives Lepke a Further Respite," *New York Times,* October 17, 1943.

23 "Roosevelt Saving Lepke Says Dewey," *New York Times,* November 27, 1943.

24 "Biddle Condemns Dewey Charge That U.S. Balks Lepke's Death," *New York Times,* November 30, 1943.

25 "State Bars Pledge to Execute Lepke," *New York Times,* December 1, 1943.

26 "Waiting For Lepke," *Newsweek,* December 13, 1943.

27 "Dewey Again Defers Execution of Three," *New York Times,* December 31, 1943.

28 "The Life of Lepke," *Newsweek,* January 3, 1944.

29 "Lepke Turned Over to the State by Biddle: Fate up to Dewey," *New York Times,* January 18, 1944.

30 "Lepke Is Turned Over to State; Placed in Sing Sing Death House," *New York Times,* January 22, 1944.

31 "New Trial Sought by Lepke," *New York Times,* January 21, 1944.

32 "Lepke Loses Plea to Get New Trial," *New York Times,* January 29, 1944.

33 Turkus and Feder, *Murder Inc.,* 412.

34 "Lepke Hearing Runs Into O'Dwyer Snag," *New York Times,* February 3, 1944.

35 "Lepke Still Hopeful; Executioner Called," *New York Times,* February 27, 1944.

36 "New Delay Looms in Lepke Execution," *New York Times,* March 1, 1944.

37 Turkus and Feder, *Murder Inc.,* 412-415.

38 Allan May, "The Last Days of 'Lepke' Buchalter," *Crime Magazine, http://crimemagazine.com/buchalter.htm,* 5-6.

39 "Lepke Fate Rests in Highest Court; Ruling Due Today," *New York Times,* March 4, 1944.

40 May, "The Last Days," 7-9.

41 "Lepke is Put to Death, Denies Guilt to Last; Makes No Revelation," *New York Times,* March 5, 1944.

42 289 NY 181, 45 NE 2d 225; *People v. Buchalter et al.,* Court of Appeals of New York, October 30, 1942, reargument denied November 25, 1942, 11.

43 Turkus and Feder, *Murder Inc.,* 417.

44 "Lepke Shows Fear As He Goes to Chair," *New York Times,* March 5, 1944.

45 Turkus and Feder, *Murder Inc.,* 415-416.

46 "Lepke and Weiss Are Buried Here," *New York Times,* March 6, 1944.

47 "Capone Laid to Rest in Gaudy Fashion," *New York Times,* March 10, 1944.

48 Walter Goodman, "Muscling In On Labor," *New Republic,* 134, April 30, 1950, 8-12.

49 Lester Velic, "Gangsters in the Dress Business," *Reader's Digest,* 67, July 1953, 59-64.

50 Goodman, "Muscling In," 8-12.

51 "What We Learned About Gangsters," *Saturday Evening Post,* May 3, 1958.

Index

Index